# Digital Business Models in

T0352798

Digital technologies are having a profound im,
opening up new opportunities to generate income and value. This
book explores the phenomenon of digitization in sport management,
with a particular focus on business models and how they are being
transformed in this new digital era.

The book explains how business models describe and underpin contemporary sport business, and how flexibility is the key to unlocking
value in an era of rapid technological change. It presents case studies
of the impact of digitization on sport organizations, in both amateur
and professional contexts, including cutting-edge topics such as the
business of football, sponsorship communication, athlete engagement, micropayments and wearable devices. The final chapter summa-
rizes current knowledge on digital business models and looks ahead at
possible future directions for sport business in the digital era.

This is fascinating reading for any advanced student, researcher or
practitioner working in sport management who wants to better understand the challenges and opportunities presented by digital technology for the sport industry.

**Mateusz Tomanek** is Assistant Professor in the Faculty of Economic Sciences and Management at the Nicolaus Copernicus University in Toruń, Poland, where he teaches management, and the
marketing of sport and wellness. He is also the chairman of the organizing committee of the International Scientific Conference *Quality in Sport* and the Editor-in-Chief of the journal *Quality in Sport*,
and local coordinator for the programme of The Governance &
Administration of Leisure and Sports International Master (GOALS)
which is financed under Erasmus Mundus Joint Master Degree.

**Wojciech Cieśliński** is Associate Professor in the Department of
Organization and Management at the Wroclaw University of Health
and Sport Sciences, Poland. He is also author of many publications in
the field of organizational space and the digitization of sport.

**Michał Polasik** is Associate Professor in the Faculty of Economic
Sciences and Management at the Nicolaus Copernicus University
in Toruń, Poland and Head of the Centre for Digital Economy and
Finance NCU. He has led several research projects regarding payment
innovations, payment systems, e-commerce, and cryptocurrencies. He
is also the co-founder and CEO of the NCU spin-off company Technology For Mobile Ltd., which aims to increase the knowledge of com-
mercialization and to cooperate with the FinTech sector.

# Routledge Research in Sport Business and Management

**Sport Officiating**
Recruitment, Development, and Retention
*Lori Livingston, Susan L. Forbes, Nick Wattie, and Ian Cunningham*

**Sport and Environmental Sustainability**
Research and Strategic Management
*Edited by Greg Dingle and Cheryl Mallen*

**Sport and the Pandemic**
Perspectives on Covid-19's Impact on the Sport Industry
*Edited by Paul M. Pedersen, Brody J. Ruihley and Bo Li*

**Embedded Multi-Level Leadership in Elite Sport**
*Edited by Svein S. Andersen, Per Øystein Hansen and Barrie Houlihan*

**Good Governance in Sport**
Critical Reflections
*Edited by Arnout Geeraert and Frank van Eekeren*

**Stakeholder Analysis and Sport Organisations**
*Edited by Anna-Maria Strittmatter, Josef Fahlén and Barrie Houlihan*

**Sport and Brexit**
Regulatory Challenges and Legacies
*Edited by Jacob Kornbeck*

**Sport Management Education**
Global Perspectives and Implications for Practice
*Edited by Mike Rayner and Tom Webb*

**Digital Business Models in Sport**
*Edited by Mateusz Tomanek, Wojciech Cieśliński and Michał Polasik*

For more information about this series, please visit https://www.routledge.com/Routledge-Research-in-Sport-Business-and-Management/book-series/RRSBM

# Digital Business Models in Sport

Edited by
**Mateusz Tomanek, Wojciech Cieśliński
and Michał Polasik**

Routledge
Taylor & Francis Group
LONDON AND NEW YORK

First published 2023
by Routledge
4 Park Square, Milton Park, Abingdon, Oxon OX14 4RN

and by Routledge
605 Third Avenue, New York, NY 10158

*Routledge is an imprint of the Taylor & Francis Group, an informa business*

*British Library Cataloguing-in-Publication Data*
A catalogue record for this book is available from the British Library

*Library of Congress Cataloging-in-Publication Data*
Names: Tomanek, Mateusz, editor. | Cieśliński, Wojciech, editor. | Polasik, Michał, editor.
Title: Digital business models in sport / edited by Mateusz Tomanek, Wojciech Cieśliński and Michał Polasik.
Identifiers: LCCN 2022008177 | ISBN 9781032218113 (hardback) | ISBN 9781032218137 (paperback) | ISBN 9781003270126 (ebook)
Subjects: LCSH: Sports administration—Data processing. | Sports—Technological innovations. | Performance technology.
Classification: LCC GV713 .D55 2022 | DDC 796.06/9—dc23/eng/20220322
LC record available at https://lccn.loc.gov/2022008177

ISBN: 978-1-032-21811-3 (hbk)
ISBN: 978-1-032-21813-7 (pbk)
ISBN: 978-1-003-27012-6 (ebk)

DOI: 10.4324/9781003270126

Typeset in Times New Roman
by codeMantra

# Contents

# Contributors

**Mikołaj Borowski-Beszta** is a PhD Candidate in the Interdisciplinary Doctoral School of Social Sciences at the Nicolaus Copernicus University, Poland. He is a participant in several team research grants and research & development projects concerning the digital economy and finance, founded by the National Science Centre and the Warsaw Institute of Banking. His main research interests include mobile banking & payments, digital services platforms, the role of wearables and alternative data exchange interfaces in retail payments.

**Marlena Ciechan-Kujawa** is Professor at the Nicolaus Copernicus University in Toruń, Poland, and an expert in improving business models, management efficiency, and creating value for the organization. She is the author of an innovative business audit model enabling multidimensional assessment of the development potential of an organization in the conditions of using a sustainable approach. Marlena is also a Member of the International Association of Controllers ICV and the Center for Leadership and Corporate Social Responsibility Council.

**Andrzej Lis** is Assistant Professor at Nicolaus Copernicus University, Poland, Executive Editor of the *Journal of Corporate Responsibility and Leadership*, and author of numerous publications in management studies. Andrzej's research focuses on knowledge management, positive organizational scholarship, corporate social responsibility, public management and logistics, sport management.

**Igor Perechuda** is Assistant Professor at LUNEX University, Luxembourg and Jagiellonian University, Poland. Igor specializes in sports clubs' management, valuation, and performance management. He has published on valuation of football clubs, and valuation of intangible assets in sports organization. He is a member of the European Accounting Association and actively supports sports business in Poland.

**Marek Siemiński** works in the Institute of Management and Quality Sciences, University of Warmia and Mazury in Olsztyn, Poland. His research areas are focused on organizational culture, corporate social responsibility, change management, and the role of value in process of management. Current projects aim to connect, role-model, and influence organizational culture, CSR, and business models.

**Adam Wiśniewski** works in the Institute of Management and Quality Sciences at University of Warmia and Mazury in Olsztyn, Poland. He is a certified sports manager and an active member of international associations. His research areas are focused on business models, sport management, entrepreneurship, value creation and strategic management. Current projects aim to develop sustainable relationships between sport results and business effectiveness and general stability of sport organizations.

# Introduction

The nature of sports organisations is to constantly adapt to changes. Most frequently, these changes concern the sports element, especially in the area of team building, which is also related to the budget available for the purchase of valuable players (not forgetting the coaching staff). An obvious activity of sports organisations is also cooperation with sponsors (finding and keeping them), which should generate a number of marketing alliances between business and sports clubs.

It is worth remembering, however, that a sports organisation is not just a professional club (for example, in Europe – a football club), playing in the highest leagues and competing for international trophies. This is important for the whole concept of business models in sport, in which the 'value' created is different for sports clubs training youth sections (the grassroots), and can also be understood differently for non-team sports (such as athletics, horse riding or sailing). Although the essence of sport is very broad in the sense that there are a multitude of competitions, most studies focus on the most popular games (*e.g.*, NBA) or disciplines (such as, for instance, football or basketball).

The sports market includes both non-profit organisations (focused on dissemination and popularisation of a given sport discipline) and for-profit organisations (sports clubs playing in professional leagues), thus the chosen business model for each organisation may be focused on different elements, of which the financial aspect will not necessarily be the most important, which is particularly visible in youth sections. However, it is necessary to be aware that in tandem with increasing levels of professionalisation in a sports club, the organisational structure, including the training staff, usually expands. There is therefore a need to generate a competitive advantage over rivals that can no longer be provided by the level of sports training alone. Increasingly, studies derived from the processing of data sets (*e.g.*, long-term biochemical and performance indicators, or analysis of the opponent's game) are

DOI: 10.4324/9781003270126-1

essential. However, such systems (digitisation) can also be implemented for youth sport, where by working with large data sets (including height, age, body mass, sports results) it is possible to adapt a sport to match the predispositions of young people.

The trend towards digital transformation of sports organisations results in a change in how they formulate their business models, but in order for that to be successful, it is important to remember that the traditional definition of a business model has to be augmented by data, information and knowledge processing methods which are an integral part of digital business models. As the Deloitte report (2021, 3) points out, sports organisations will have to invest in multi-channel digital solutions so that they can also be open to virtual fans (*e.g.*, creating streaming platforms, building applications using augmented and virtual reality).

Sznajder (2020, 5–6), citing the results of Vailati Facchini (2018), notes that the digitisation of sport mainly concerns two areas: (1) impact on athletes' performance, e.g. game analysis, rehabilitation of athletes, and (2) club management of sports). In these areas, digital technologies can be used, among other things, for the following purposes: managing a club team (creating a team for a specific sports event), infrastructure and safety management, acquiring sports talent, and sponsorship. In addition to these two main areas, the authors add that it is important to focus the digitisation of sport on (3) sports event management and (4) building fan experiences.

In connection with the challenges for sports organisations created by the digital transformation process, this publication has been prepared with the aim of explaining how and why business models are developed. The first chapter introduces the reader to the concept of business models (citing more than 70 definitions) and their trends. The authors (Adam Wiśniewski and Marek Siemiński) start by defining the role of values as a key aspect in the creation of business models. The authors also refer to the sports sphere, where sport values are defined in four sub-dimensions (Nam-Ik, Sun-Mun, 2017): physical, aesthetic, emotional and social. The second chapter, authored by Andrzej Lis describes the mapping of research fields in the area of business models in sport. Based on the Scopus database, only 182 publications in this area have been identified, but not a single one refers to mapping and profiling. Analysing the texts with the help of VOSviewer software, it was noted that the prevailing research fronts relate to the following areas: business models of football clubs, business models of amateur/ non-profit sports clubs, business models of sports organisations in the COVID-19 context, business models of electronic sports.

After presenting the most important information about business models in sport (Chapters 1 and 2), the next section of the book covers the definition of digital business models, which the authors (Wojciech Cieśliński and Mateusz Tomanek) define as the use of modern digital tools and social media to stream **value** flows (real-time flows of data, information and knowledge), the use of these tools to implement gamification mechanisms (real-time assessment of the effectiveness of sports behaviour during sports training, competition and the media value of the event). The next chapter, written by Adam Wiśniewski, presents the essence of the concept of flexibility in building business models. Here we read that despite the basic activity of a sports club, which is conducting training or preparing a team for participation in sports competitions, few possibilities exist for a flexible process approach using digital resources. However, there is a greater opportunity to exploit flexibility in the commercial sports market. The first pathway to training delivery (such as, for instance, fitness clubs) can be used in a simple subscription model or a direct-to-customer (D2C) model. In both cases, the training unit can be offered using the Internet. An amateur athlete, in order to train, could purchase a subscription (or access) to a digital platform with a training programme so that they can train anywhere in the world. The direct-to-customer model offers individual solutions for each athlete, including live broadcast supervision and consultation services.

The business models adopted by sports organisations are influenced not only by the owners/management, but also by sports associations (national and international ones). The next chapter (by Marlena Ciechan-Kujawa and Igor Perechuda) describes an example of how the Financial Fair Play (FFP) regulations introduced in the 2013/2014 season by UEFA changed the parameters of economic policy and the principles of a sustainable approach to the activities of football clubs.

While the previous chapters focus more on team sports and the use of digital business models in them, it should be noted that digital transformation is not just for them. There is also a great potential for the use of digitisation in the area of individual sports, including its use by organisations creating, for example, amateur running events. In the final chapter Mikołaj Borowski-Beszta and Michał Polasik describe the use of wearable devices in the context of financial services. It is worth noting that this type of activity not only facilitates the purchasing process, but also enables sports event organisers to become more involved in sponsorship cooperation with financial sector institutions.

## References

Deloitte, (2021). *2021 Outlook for the US sports industry*. Deloitte Center for Technology, Media & Telecommunications.

Nam-Ik, K., Sun-Mun, P. (2017). The relationship between media sports involvement experiences and sports values and sports participation. *International Journal of Applied Engineering Research*, 12 (20), 9768–9773.

Sznajder A. (2020). Technologie informacyjno-komunikacyjne w marketingu sportu. ICT information and communication technologies in sport marketing. *Marketing i Rynek/ Journal of Marketing and Market Studies*, XXVII, no 3. doi:10.33226/1231-7853.2020.3.1

Vailati Facchini, L. (2018). *Digital strategy of a sport club: A model to support the analysis*. Politecnico di Milano. https://www.politesi.polimi.it/bitstream/ 10589/139278/3/2018_04_VailatiFacchini.pdf

# 1 Business Models Trends in Sport

*Adam Wiśniewski and Marek Siemiński*

## Introduction

In analyzing structures for the creation of new business models or the modification of existing ones, it is essential to understand the context of the changes taking place. Each sector of the economy has its own, different conditions that influence the business models applied. Similarly, within a given sector there are different component parts which influence and determine the way an organization functions.

It is no different within what is broadly termed sport, from professional sports to those operating at a lower level of professionalization. Consequently, it is interesting to identify what features constitute a common, universal area of contemporary decision-makers' behavior in building or adjusting a business model. This chapter presents an overview of selected contemporary decision-making priorities in the business models of sports organizations.

## Value as the starting point of a business model in sport

To discuss this in detail, we necessarily begin with a basic explanation of the business model concept and its priorities. The starting point for any business model is the definition of what the customer expects and what is offered by the organization. All the elements the customer expects represent some kind of value for him or her. The customer is therefore willing to pay the acquisition cost to receive that value. On the other hand, a company's offer is valued by the buyer through the prism of her individual perception of this value. Value is always uniquely and phenomenologically determined by the beneficiary (Vargo, Lush 2008, p. 8).

DOI: 10.4324/9781003270126-2

## Essence of value

Values are generally defined as principles or standards that are considered worthwhile or desirable (MacLean, Hamm, 2008). As underlined by many authors point out, values help to select and evaluate behaviors, define goals, and set standards for acceptable behavior (Lee et al., 2000). J. Petri and F. Jacob (2017) define value perception issues in three dimensions: customer as locus of value creation, relational value creation, and value as dependent on perception. Value is the result of the customer experience (Figure 1.1).

From these points of view there emerges the perspective that value is always uniquely and phenomenologically determined by the beneficiary (Vargo, Lusch, 2008). But it is worth noting that the key aspect is the relation between value and firms' structure or management. This 'creation', understood as a product, relates to both physical product and services as businesses' main output. From the buyer's perspective, as already stated, value is what they are willing to pay for. We will now focus on this area and try to explain the basic areas of value to the customer (Figure 1.1).

Value is expressed in four basic dimensions (Wiśniewski, 2021):

- value proposition – the logic of business activities focused on creating value for customers and/or stakeholders by offering a product and providing services that meet needs;

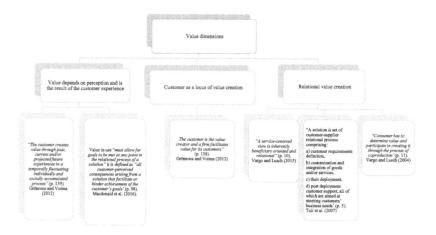

*Figure 1.1* Dimensions of value perception.
Source: Own research based on: Petri, J., Jacob, F. (2017).

- value architecture – the construction of an organization with a technological and organizational structure to enable the volume of products and services and the flow of information;
- value network – the way in which an organization enables transactions through coordination and collaboration between transacting parties and external parties;
- financial value – how the organization addresses cost, price, and revenue fluctuations to keep it stable and growing.

There are many definitions of value. It is identified as the difference between the sum of all benefits for the customer and all the costs to them of choosing one organization's offer over others (Kotler, 2005). Another familiar definition underlines the difference between the buyer's willingness to pay and the opportunity cost (Brandenburger, Stuart jr. 1996). Most definitions are based on a company's offering and its features.

Two main categories of value can be distinguished (Smith, 1954): exchangeability and use. The first defines the willingness to exchange one thing for another. It determines what level of 'acceptance' will realize the exchange. Use value, on the other hand, defines the level of satisfaction with which needs are met by a product or service.

The main categories of value identified by the recipients include emotional, economic, technical, and social values. *Emotional values* are linked to the feelings the recipient experiences. Thus, a given object can evoke pleasure, be beautiful to the recipient, or draw on deeper feelings, such as love. *Economic values* are derived from transaction characteristics. Here, the customer pays attention to price, terms of the transaction, availability of the product, and elements related to delivery (e.g., cost or time). *Technical values* are based on the characteristics of the product. The buyer takes into account whether it is durable, useful or easy to use. *Social values*, on the other hand, are related to the influence purchasing the product has on environment. We can distinguish between environmental impact, change in the user's way of life and the company's responsibility for the product or service.

The general assumption of manufacturers is that the greater the bundle of values with which the product is 'encased' the more the customer is willing to pay to purchase it. The value categories outlined above are a universal set, used in every sector of the economy. However, it is worth noting that some sectors accentuate other value category structures or even have unique values not relevant to the rest of the economy. For example, Van Wart (1998) discusses values in the public sector, based on the Code of Ethics redrafted by ASPA's Professional

Ethics Committee and its subcommittee. Code of Ethics identifies five sources related to personal/individual, professional, organizational, legal, and public interest values. In discussing *personal/individual values*, the author based his discussion on integrity, defined as 'the state of being complete, unbroken condition, wholeness' (*Webster's New...,* 1978). Integrity is based on four characteristics (Van Wart, 1998, *Changing Public Sector Values,* Routledge, p. 5):

- honesty - without integrity there can be no proper communication;
- consistcy - action should be based on principles and not on impulse or the moment;
- coherence - principles should be combined with their examples to make them as harmonious as possible;
- reciprocity - we should behave towards others as we would like them to behave towards us in similar conditions and situations.

*Professional values* should enhance the abilities of individuals and encourage personal growth. They are based on four principles:

1  providing support and incentives to improve competence.
2  acceptance of personal responsibility for priority issues and emerging problems.
3  encouraging others, throughout their careers, to participate in professional activities and associations.
4  having time to meet and build bridges between individuals and the organization.

*Organizational values* indicate the most distinctive and definite characteristics of an institution (Williams, 1979). They are beliefs and attitudes that reach inside the organization and represent a collective understanding of the norms and standards of behavior accepted in it (Hassan, 2007). Organizational values serve multiple purposes. They set the tone for the environment, bring people together, facilitate work function, and achieve common goals. They also represent shared ambitions because values define who and what each person has to offer as a human being to the entire enterprise (Mirabile, 1996).

*Legal values* can be broadly defined as laws, local and national; rules and regulations that define how things work. *Public interest values* are based on the definition of public interest. Van Wart (1998) defines it as encouraging open government and continuous communication with the public, which may be necessary as a result of the public's unawareness of its needs or poor adaptation to the use of public institutions. In this perspective, the involvement of the public in the administration is promoted whenever possible, for example by using public forums or citizens' councils.

Specific values can similarly be identified in the sport sector but before discussing them, it is important to highlight the differences between amateur and professional sport. Despite these differences, it is also possible to see values that are common to both categories. Czechowski (2015) emphasizes the autotelic nature of sport values and defines their categories:

- an enduring element of a healthy lifestyle,
- a chance for self-realization,
- orientation towards proper social communication,
- subjectivity in an approach to a pupil,
- reference to respect, trust, and dialogue,
- a symbol of development and life,
- striving for control over one's own body,
- a state of well-being and a chance to be with others in leisure,
- a source of joy in life.

Sports values can be defined in four 'sub-variables' (Nam-Ik, Sun-Mun, 2017): physical, aesthetic, emotional, and social. In general sport values represent the principles that guide behavior and support individual decision-making in various situations in sport (Lee et al., 2013). Gonçalves (2017) describes three domains of sport values:

1 moral values – represent the valuing of the moral aspects of an event.
2 status – team or individual prioritizes winning and gaining social recognition.
3 competence – referred to values associated with continuous striving for greater competence in sport.

Nascimento Jr et al. (2021) noted that sport can be connected to some processes of character formation and moral development, and that this also underlines its importance for encouraging positive social behavior (Kavussanu, Stanger, 2017). Adell et al. (2019) conducted a study that confirmed the transfer of personal values to values in sport and linked them to attitudes in games development. They also highlighted that moral attitudes (both pro- and anti-social) are directly and indirectly observable in sport values (such as those connected to competence and status) and through goal orientation.

In the case of sports organizations, including sports clubs, the values generated are more broadly represented to potential customers than they are in classic businesses. With the skillful use of resources, it is possible to increase the productivity and profitability of the club and increase value.

## Essence of business models

The starting point for any business model is the skillful definition of value. Various aspects and categories of value should be taken into account here, as mentioned earlier. It is also worth emphasizing value flow direction. On the one hand the organization prepares value for the buyer. On the other hand, the proposed offer contains a bundle of value captured by the company. This bundle forms the basis for the company's livelihood as well as profit generation. Over the years, dozens of business model definitions have been created. Depending on their perspective, they emphasize different features or priorities relevant to a particular organization. The most popular business model definitions are presented below (Table 1.1).

In analyzing this list, a recurring emphasis on the priority of creating value and the necessity of using available resources and ways of functioning of the whole organization become visible. These are so important that they contributes to the verification of contemporary business models and to the individual search for improvement solutions for particular elements. On the one hand, there is no single, universally used definition of a business model. On the other hand, perhaps the most widely cited definition is that of Osterwalder and Pigneur (2010) who state that a business model 'rationally describes how an organization creates, delivers, and captures value'. Taking this definition as a reference point, the universalist property of the business model can be confirmed, and also applied to the sports sector.

Modern companies face the problem of market oversaturation and are additionally limited by the occurrence of recessions or economic problems in a given market. Fullerton and Morgan (2009) highlighted the importance of the impact of the recession in reducing sports marketing activities. They noted that manufacturers of 'non-sports products began to avoid the sports sector' while at the same time noting the opportunities associated with reorganization, downsizing, product deletion, and the use of media, including the Internet, to communicate with audiences. M. Goldman (2011) did a detailed analysis of the impact of the recession on Sports Marketing Business Model Shifts (Table 1.2).

*Table 1.1* Business model definitions

| No. | Author | Definition |
|---|---|---|
| | Brandenburger, Stuart (1996) | The business model defines the organization's approach to generating revenue at a reasonable cost and embodies assumptions about creating and capturing value. |
| | Boulton et al. (1997) | A business model is a unique combination of tangible and intangible assets that create an organization's ability to create value. |
| | Timmers (1998) | A business e-model is an architecture for products, services, and information streams that includes a description of the various business activities and their roles. |
| | Vankatraman, Henderson (1998) | A business model is a coordinated plan to design a strategy along three vectors: customer interaction, asset configuration, and knowledge enhancement. |
| | Slywotzky et al. (2000) | An enterprise business model is a compact and mutually reinforcing whole. It should be customer-centric. |
| | Hamel (2000) | A business model is a customer-related composition of key strategy, strategic resources, and value networks. |
| | Linder, Cantrell (2000) | The business model is the core logic of an organization about value creation. |
| | Boulton et al. (2001) | A business model is a portfolio of assets resulting from their unique combination. |
| | Weil, Vitale (2001) | A business model provides a description of the roles and relationships among the consumers, customers, allies, and suppliers of a business enabling identification of the major product, information, and money streams and the major benefits to the participants. |
| | Amit, Zott (2001) | The business model outlines the essence, structure, and direction of transactions to create value by capitalizing on business opportunities. |
| | Amit, Zott (2001) | A [business model is a] system of interconnected and interdependent activities that defines how you do business with your customers, partners, and suppliers. |
| | Applegate (2001) | A business model is a description of the complexity of a business that explores its structure, the relationships between structural elements, and how the business will respond in the real world. The structure of the business model is based on the organization's industry logic. |
| | Afuah, Tucci (2001) | A business model is a system of interrelated elements that interact with each other over time. |

*(Continued)*

| No. | Author | Definition |
|---|---|---|
| | Porter (2001) | A business model is a general concept of operation. |
| | Magretta (2002) | Business models are stories that explain how business ventures work. They describe how resources are combined and transformed to generate value for the customer and other stakeholders, and how the business generating the value will be rewarded by the stakeholders receiving it. |
| | Sandberg (2002) | The business model identifies the levers to carry out the strategy and the norms and assumptions that help you move along the chosen path. |
| | Hoque (2002) | The business model captures a picture of the enterprise and communicates the direction and goals to the stakeholders of the enterprise. |
| | Osterwalder, Pigneur (2002) | A business model is the conceptual and architectural implementation of a business strategy and the basis for introducing business processes. It contains the enterprise's value proposition to one or more customer segments and the architecture of the enterprise and its network of partners to create value and relationship capital to generate profitable and sustainable revenue streams. |
| | Chesbrough and Rosenbloom (2002) | The business model articulates the value proposition, identifies the market segment, defines value chain structures, calculates cost structures and potential profits, describes the company's position in the value chain linking suppliers, the company and customers, and formulates a competitive strategy to retain profits. |
| | Obłój (2002) | A business model is a total concept of an enterprise operation. It is a combination of a strategic concept and the technology of its practical implementation, understood as the construction of a value chain that allows effective exploitation and renewal of resources and skills. |
| | Afuah, Tucci (2003) | A business model is a method adopted by a company to augment and leverage its resources to present customers with product and service offerings that are superior to those of its competitors while ensuring the company's profitability. It is a complex system with interrelated elements that interact with each other over time. Its essence lies in specifying how the enterprise is to make money in the long run. |

| | |
|---|---|
| Hedman, Kalling (2003) | The business model combines internal aspects that transform factors into resources through the activity of industrial forces to produce products offered to the market. For a business to be able to manage industrial forces and serve marketable products, it needs access to the market for factors (capital, labor) and raw materials. |
| Mitchell, Coles (2003) | Business model means improvement and change. It includes the combined elements describing: "who", "what", "when", "why", "where", "how", and "how much" it captures in delivering products and services to customers and end users. |
| Howe (2004) | A business model captures the unique activity an organization needs to undertake externally to accomplish its mission, serve its customers, and generate revenue. |
| Yip (2004) | The business model includes the target customer, the nature of the business, and how revenue will be generated (now and in the future). |
| Bossidy, Charan (2004) | A business model is a combination of external environment, internal operations (especially strategy) and financial objectives. It brings rationality to the realm of change by indicating what to change and when. |
| Banaszyk (2004) | A business model is a more or less developed idea of the desired development of a company and its conditions. |
| Rappa (2004) | A business model describes the method of "doing" business. It details what the business does to create value, its place in the value chain, and its relationship with customers to generate revenue. |
| Seddon et al. (2004) | A business model describes the fundamental details of the value proposition and the systems of operations that a business uses to create and deliver value to its customers. |
| Morris et al. (2004) | The business model captures what the business system will focus on. It is a concise representation of the related components of strategic business decisions, architecture, and economics addressed to create sustainable competitive advantages in defined markets. |

(*Continued*)

| No. | Author | Definition |
|---|---|---|
| | Osterwalder et al. (2005) | A business model is a conceptual tool that expresses the business logic of an enterprise and contains a set of objects, concepts, and their relationships to a goal. It captures the description of: value directed to one or more customer segments, the architecture of the company, the network of partners in value creation, the means of value delivery, relational capital, and sustainable revenue streams. The components of the business model are key activities, key partners, key resources, cost structure, customer relationships, customer segments, value proposition, channels, and revenue streams. |
| | Rokita (2005) | The business model reflects the means of achieving appropriate economic performance expressed by the relationships of revenue, cost, and profit across the organization. The business model corresponds directly to the performance model. |
| | Kim, Mauborgne (2005) | No direct definition. A business model is a customer value proposition derived from utility and price. |
| | Business Model Alchemist (2005) | A business model is nothing more than a description of an organization making (or wanting to make) money. |
| | Shah et al. (2005) | The business model defines the revenue generation proposition. Income generation involves the combination of information and services. |
| | Romanowska (2005) | A business model is the method of acquiring customers and serving them that has been adopted for a particular sector. |
| | Voelpel et al. (2005) | A business model is the concept of indigenous values offered to customers and the configuration of a value delivery network consisting of the company's own strategic capabilities and other values in that network (e.g., outsourcing, alliances) and the company's continuous effort to change and satisfy stakeholder objectives. |
| | Shafer et al. (2005) | A business model is a representation of a company's core logic and strategic choices for creating and capturing value. |
| | Malone et al. (2006) | Business models capture what companies do and how they create value. |
| | Muszyński (2006) | A business model is the way in which a company makes a profit. |

| | |
|---|---|
| Brzóska (2007) | The strategic model of an energy company is a combination of the concept of competitive advantage with a set of activities and resources necessary for its implementation, enabling the organization (company) to achieve its intended objectives, including in particular profitability and contributing to energy security. |
| Chesbrough (2007a, 2007b) | The business model describes the creation and acquisition of value. |
| Witt, Meyer (2007) | A business system used by a company is a composition of resources (input), activities (processing), and products or services offered (final product) to create value for customers. |
| Maxwell, Rankin (2007) | A business model is a conceptual model that identifies what you do and how you create value. It describes: how you make money, how you deliver your solutions, and how you generate money for other people. |
| Neely, Delbridge (2007) | The ideal business model: draws a line around what you do, sketches how it is done, explains how to link internal processes with external customer requirements and strategic goals. |
| Johnson et al. (2008) | A business model harmonizes four interconnected elements that together create and deliver value. These are: revenue model, cost structure, margin model and resource rotation. |
| Nielsen, Bukh (2008) | The overall business model can be defined as either a meta-model or an ontology for the business model, e.g. a meta-model forms the basis for a business model by specifying: the features of an enterprise's thinking, its operating system, and its ability to generate value. A broadly defined business model captures suggestions in light of the entire enterprise regarding its elements and their combinations that enable value creation. |
| Gołębiowski et al. (2008) | A business model is a new conceptual tool containing a set of elements and relations between them, which represent the logic of activity of a given enterprise in a given field (business). It includes a description of the value offered by an enterprise to a group or groups of customers, together with an identification of the primary resources, processes (activities) and external relationships of that enterprise to create, offer and deliver that value, and ensure that the enterprise is competitive in its field and can increase its value. |

*(Continued)*

| No. | Author | Definition |
|---|---|---|
| | Jabłoński (2008) | Business model is understood as a mapping in a given place, time, and business space of the structure of interrelationships of factors that ensure the fulfillment of current, internal and external needs of stakeholder groups, which enables the current achievement of competitive advantage by the company and is the creation of a future platform for growth and development of the company, ensuring continuity of business. |
| | Nogalski (2009) | A business model is a general concept that formulates a framework for the logic of doing business and its characteristics such as innovation or competitiveness. |
| | Lisein et al. (2009) | The business model describes three axes: who the customers are and what type of customers the business is specifically targeting, what are the products/services offered by the enterprise, what are the needs they are willing to buy, how the enterprise distributes its products and how it eludes competitors to supply its products. |
| | Board of Innovation (2009) | The business model is communicated through its parts: Part 1 - the players (enterprise, consumer), Part 2 - the flow from the enterprise to the customer (product, service, experience, reputation), Part 3 - the flow from the customer to the enterprise (money, other benefits, customer attention, disclosure, and dissemination of product advantages). |
| | Kujala et al. (2010) | Business models combine perspectives on strategy, company relationships, and company operations. Specifically, business models grow out of creating value for the customer. |
| | Itami, Nishino (2010) | The business model is seen as consisting of two elements – the business system and the revenue model. |
| | Rappa (2010) | A business model is a method of "doing" business so that a company can sustain itself by generating revenue. |
| | Kotelnikov (2010) | A business model is an "umbrella" covering the method of doing business. The method consists of the position in the value chain, customer selection, products and pricing. |

| | |
|---|---|
| Smith et al. (2010) | Business model refers to the idea by which an organization converts strategic choices - about markets, customers, value proposition - and uses the specific architecture of the organization – people, competencies, processes, culture, and measurement systems – to create and capture that value. |
| Niemczyk (2010) | A business model is a mix of strategy, tactics, and operations that is the key to success in a specific group of businesses at a given time. |
| Bossidy, Charan (2010) | A business model describes a holistic, extended, and grounded in reality process of thinking about specific elements of running a business. It shows how to link together the financial goals necessary to achieve the external conditions in which the business operates, as well as such internal processes as strategy development, operational tactics, and employee selection and development. |
| Wikström et al. (2010) | Business models describe the value creation chain, the streams, and constellations of value between diverse business actors. |
| Kondström (2010) | The business model offers a useful structure for analyzing and understanding the business and its parts, reducing imitability and the importance of consistency between the business strategy and all of its structural elements. |
| Casadesus-Masanell, Ricart (2010) | A business model indicates the "logic of a company" describing how it operates and creates value for its stakeholders. It reflects an understanding of the company's strategy. The business model is about how a company identifies and creates value for customers and captures some of that value as revenue. |
| Osterwalder, Pigneur (2010) | A business model rationally describes how an organization creates, delivers, and captures value. |
| Demil, Lecocq (2010) | In the statistical approach, a business model is a photocopy of the coherence between its core components. In the transformational (dynamic) approach, it is a tool for change and innovation either in the organization or in the model itself. An organization's business model is a snapshot, at a given time, of the ongoing interactions between the core components. |

(*Continued*)

| No. | Author | Definition |
|-----|--------|-----------|
| | Teece (2010) | The business model articulates the logic of how the business creates and delivers value to customers. It also defines the revenue, cost, and benefit architecture associated with the business delivering that value. The business model defines how the business creates and delivers value to customers and how it transforms the compensation received into profit. |
| | Sceulovs et al. (2011) | The business model describes its components (including metrics, processes, technology, and workforce). |
| | Sorescu et al. (2011) | The business model represents the distinctive logic of the company for value creation and capture. It is a well-articulated system of interdependent structures [and] fields of activity and serves to transform the organization's logic for creating value for its customers and appropriating value for itself and its partners. |
| | Cyfert, Krzakiewicz (2011) | A business model defines the logic of relations between resources available to an organization and activities that create value for its customers. |
| | Eyring et al. (2012) | A business model is constructed by combining four components: customer value proposition, profit formula, key processes and resources. |
| | Arend (2013) | A business model is defined as a useful representation of how an organization creates value by transforming and transferring matter using available factors and driven by identified economic power. |
| | Baden-Fuller, Mangematin (2013) | A business model provides a "manipulable instrument" that can be used to examine cause and effect and to better understand the business world. |
| | Buur et al. (2013) | A business model is a simplified presentation of a company's business logic: it describes how it "makes" money through its products or services. |
| | Johnson (2013) | The business model defines how an organization creates value for the customer and simultaneously builds value for itself. |
| | Falencikowski (2013) | A business model is a relatively isolated, conceptual multicomponent object describing the arrangement of a for-profit enterprise that, through structures, emerges the logic of how value is created for the customer and captured by the enterprise. |
| | Bocken et al. (2014) | The business model is defined by three main elements of value: its proposition, creation and capture. |

| Brzóska (2014) | The business model can be regarded as some new, developed form of the organizational (management) model of the enterprise. It refers to the strategy at the corporate level. In it, the basic variables of the enterprise organization sphere are defined at a general level by activities and resources. The model does not capture the details of organizational structure or power distribution - typical of classical organizational models. |
|---|---|

Source: Own research based on: Wiśniewski A. (2021), *Modele biznesu klubów piłki siatkowej. W drodze do zwiększania konkurencyjności.* Wydawnictwo Uniwersytetu Warmińsko-Mazurskiego w Olsztynie.

*Table 1.2* Recession-driven business model shifts

| Pre-recession business model | Value proposition defined by media exposure and supporter numbers. | Highly competitive independent agencies that do not work together. | Middle-man commissions-based revenues. | Employees characterized by previous athletes with strong relationships. |
|---|---|---|---|---|
| Recession-triggered business model | Value proposition defined by measurable business value outcomes. | Competitive, but increasingly collaborative arrangements. | Consulting on project-based revenues. | Employees increasingly characterized as business and marketing graduates. |

Source: Own research based on: Goldman, M. M. (2011).

It is clear that recession is forcing changes, leading to more effective management of organizations as well as all outward-facing activities. A positive impact of digital activities, focused on competitiveness, is visible (Ferreira et al., 2019). Established businesses must embrace innovation and modify their digital infrastructure to effectively integrate digital technologies into day-to-day operation of their organizations (Warner, Wager, 2019). As a result, their business models are being exposed to the challenges of digital innovation (Do Vale et al. 2021). We can see two basic trends of change and priorities in business models in sports: innovations and digitization. We will characterize each of these priorities below. As these priorities often intersect or co-mingle (Figure 1.2), they will be discussed together, reflecting the logical structure of their interconnectedness. This is especially true

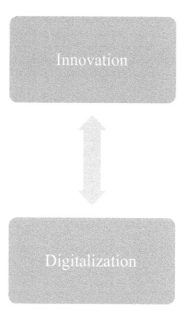

*Figure 1.2* The pattern of cross-calling business model priorities.
Source: Own research.

for the priority of digitization, which is often the launching point for innovation in business models.

The issue of *innovation* has been studied and discussed in depth over the past decades. Significantly, according to studies, more than 60% of innovation projects in the economy are related to digitization (Asko, 2006). As shown in the IBM survey of 2009, 7 out of 10 companies surveyed implemented innovations in their business models and as many as 98% made various modifications to them (Bis, 2013). It is highly advisable for sports clubs to use value proposition as a potential area for business model innovation (Heck, 2021).

## Conclusions

As Dima (2015) states in relation to the soccer industry, it is changing on a daily basis and clubs have to innovate new models despite these developments. 'European soccer has completely changed especially in the last 20 years, following a major cycle of trading and marketing, a cycle that has brought in significant wholesale amounts of cash'

(p. 1245). The adoption of digital technologies in sport has triggered changes in the way sport itself is received and has increased levels of interactivity (Ratten, 2020). J. Kay (2006), listing the distinctive capabilities of the enterprise, mentions its architecture as a factor that makes it flexible and capable of adapting to changes in the environment. This means that clubs need to change and innovate.

New solutions enable stronger audience engagement. Z. Waśkowski and A. Jasiulewicz (2021), discussing the seventh PKO Białystok Half-Marathon, drew attention to new technological solutions in communication with athletes. 'Digital technologies have given runners the opportunity to engage electronically in all phases of the event. Moreover, the multitude of digital solutions in that sports event provided new value, 'making the runners become prosumers of the event (i.e. its active co-creators), and not only its users' (p. 1136). Researchers on the impact of digital innovation in sport have taken a similar line. 'Digital innovation has profoundly changed the different modalities of interaction of the world of sport with their fans' (Iannella, Morandini, 2016, p. 25). They also point out the benefits of using digital innovation in sports:

- technology helps monitor values originally impossible to record with physical observation,
- the quality of coaching is improved through structured processes supported by technology,
- the best solutions are adaptable to the requirements of a specific audience,
- digital platforms support the exchange of information and data and the achievement of the so-called big picture.

Analyzing trends in the changing functioning of sports clubs and organizations reveals an analogy with traditional business and it is important to note the convergence of changes in flexibility with the digitization of primarily channels of communication with an audience. The analogy is particularly evident where organizations provide services.

Technological progress and the acceleration of change caused, for example, by pandemics have forced changes in the business models of sports entities. The greatest pressure has come from the fear of losing loyal customers and the desire to interest them in new distribution channels. Of particular interest are questions around the sustainability of the changes taking place seem. Will organizations maintain the modifications they have introduced, or will they abandon them, e.g. due to maintenance costs? Regardless of global and regional conditions, the need for change in the competition for customers seems a certainty.

# Bibliography

Adell, F.L., Alvarez, O., Castillo I. (2019). Personal and sport values, goal orientations and moral attitudes in youth basketball, *Journal of Sport Psychology*, 28 (1), 104–105.

Afuah, A.N., Tucci, C. (2001). Internet business models and strategies. Text and cases. *McGraw-Hill/Irwin*, New York.

Afuah, A.N., Tucci, C. (2003). Biznes internetowy. Strategie i modele. *Oficyna Ekonomiczna* (pp. 1–545), Kraków.

Amit, R., Zott, C. (2001). Value creation in e-business, *Strategic Management Journal*, 22.

Applegate, L.M. (2001). E-business models. Making sense of the Internet business landscape [in:] Dickson, G., DeSanctis, G. (eds.) *Information technology and the future enterprise. New models for managers*, Prentice-Hall, New York.

Arend, R.J. (2013). The business model. Present and future – beyond a skeumorph, *Strategic Organisation*, 36.

Baden-Fuller, Ch., Mangematin, V. (2013). Business models. A challenging agenda, *Strategic Organisation*, 422.

Banaszyk, P. (2004). Model biznesu jako podstawa zarządzania strategicznego przedsiębiorstwem [in:] Urbanowska-Sojkin, E., Banaszyk, P. (eds) Współczesne metody zarządzania strategicznego przedsiębiorstwem. *Wydawnictwo Akademii Ekonomicznej w Poznaniu*, Poznań, pp. 16.

Bis, J. (2013). Innowacyjny model biznesowy – sposób na zwiększenie przewagi konkurencyjnej, [in:] Kożuch B. (et al.). Modele biznesowe. *Wydawnictwo Społecznej Akademii Nauk w Łodzi*, pp. 54.

Bocken, N.M.P., Short, S.W., Rana, P., Evans, S. (2014). A literature and practice review to develop sustainable business model archetypes. *Journal of Cleaner Production*, 43.

Board of Innovation, http://www.boardofinnovation.com/howbuildanybusinessmodelwithon- ly10blocks, access: 12.03.2022.

Bossidy, L., Charan, R. (2004). Business supermodels. What should you change and what should you keep in your organization? "CIO", November 15, vol. 18, iss. 4.

Bossidy, L., Charan, R. (2010). *Szósty zmysł w zarządzaniu firmą. Tworzenie wykonalnych planów i modeli biznesowych,* MT Biznes Sp. z o.o., Warszawa.

Boulton, R.E.S., Libert, B.D., Samek, S.M. (1997). Cracking the value code. How successful businesses are creating wealth in the new economy, *Harper Collins Publishers*, New York.

Boulton, R.E.S., Libert, B.D., Samek, S.M. (2001). *Odczytując kod wartości,* WIG-Press, Warszawa.

Brandenburger, A.M., Stuart H.W. (1996). Value-based business strategy, *Journal of Economics & Management Strategy*, 5, 10.

Brzóska, J. (2007). *Modele strategiczne przedsiębiorstw energetycznych,* Wydawnictwo Politechniki Śląskiej, Gliwice.

Brzóska, J. (2014). Innowacje jako czynnik dynamizujący modele biznesowe. *Wydawnictwo Politechniki Śląskiej,* Gliwice.

Buur, J., Ankenband, B., Mitchell, R. (2013). Participatory business modeling, *CoDesign*, 9(1), 55.

Casadesus-Masanell, R., Ricart, J.E. (2010). From strategy to business models and onto tactics, *Long Range Planning*, nr 43, 201.

Chesbrough, H. (2007a). Business model innovation, it's not just about technology anymore, *Strategy & Leadership*, 35, 13.

Chesbrough, H. (2007b). Why companies should have open business models? *MIT Sloan Management Review*, 48, 3.

Chesbrough, H., Rosenbloom, R. (2002). The Role of business model in capturing value from innovations. Evidence from Xerox Corporation's technology spin-off companies, *Industrial Corporate Change*, 11 (3), 5.

Cyfert, S., Krzakiewicz, K. (2011). Wykorzystanie koncepcji modeli biznesu w zasobowej teorii firmy, [w:] Rozwój szkoły zasobowej zarządzania strategicznego, *Prace Naukowe Wałbrzyskiej Wyższej Szkoły Zarządzania i Przedsiębiorczości*. Wałbrzych.

Czechowski, J. (2015). Sport w perspektywie procesu wychowawczego. *Przegląd pedagogiczny*, 2, 161–178.

Demil, B., Lecocq, X. (2010). Business model evolution. In search of dynamic consistency, *Long Range Planning*, nr 43, 228.

Dima, T. (2015). The business model of European football club competitions. *Procedia Economics and Finance*, 23, 1245–1252. doi:10.1016/S2212–5671(15) 00562-6.

Do Vale, G., Collin-Lachaud, I., Lecocq, X. (2021). Micro-level practices of bricolage during business model innovation process: The case of digital transformation towards omni-channel retailing, *Scandinavian Journal of Management*, 37 (2), 11.

Esko, A. (2006). Creating an Innovative Europe (access: 23.08.2021) http://www.kigeit.org.pl/ftp/IUSER/Literatura/068%20Creating%20an%20innovative%20Europe_Aho_report.pdf

Eyring, M.J., Johnson, M.W., Nair, H. (2012). Nowe modele biznesowe. Sposób na podbój rynków wschodzących, *Harvard Business Review Polska*, pp. 96.

Falencikowski, T. (2013). *Spójność modeli biznesu. Koncepcja i pomiar.* Wydawnictwo CeDeWu, Warszawa.

Ferreira, J.J.M., Fernandes, C.I., Ferreira, F.A.F. (2019). To be or not to be digital, that is the question: firm innovation and performance, *Journal of Business Research*, 101, 583–590.

Fullerton, S., Morgan, M.J. (2009). Sports marketing in an economic quagmire. Paper presented at the 7th Annual Sport Marketing Association Conference, 28–30 October, Cleveland, OH.

Goldman, M.M. (2011). Post-crisis sports marketing business model shifts. *Managing Global Transitions,* 9 (2), 171–184.

Gołębiowski Tadeusz, Dudzik Teresa Magdalena, Witek-Hajduk Małgorzata Marzanna. (2008). Modele biznesu polskich przedsiębiorstw. *Szkoła Główna Handlowa w Warszawie*, Warszawa.

Gonçalves, John (2017). *Sport Builds Character: A Critical Assessment of Moral Reasoning and Development in Sport*. Academia Publishing, pp. 16.

Grönroos, C., Voima, P. (2012). Critical service logic: making sense of value creation and co-creation, *Journal of the Academy of Marketing Science*, 41 (2), 133–150. doi:10.1007/s11747-012-0308-3

Hamel, G. (2000). *Leading the revolution*, Harvard Business School Press, Boston.

Hassan, A. (2007). Human resource development and organizational values, *Journal of European Industrial Training*, 31 (6), 435–448.

Heck, L. (2021). Rethinking the business model of FC Bayern Munich Basketball. *Final Master Thesis at Vytautas Magnus University in Kaunas*.

Hedman, J., Kalling, T. (2003). The business model concept. Theoretical underpinnings and empirical illustrations, *European Journal of Information Systems*, nr 12, 50.

Hoque, F. (2002). The Alignment Effect. How to get real business value out of technology, *Financial Times*, Prentice Hall.

Howe, P.E. (2004). Business models, *Pennsylvania CPA Journal*, nr 74. Iannella, F., Morandini, A. (2016). Digital innovation in the sport industry: The case of athletic performance. *Master Thesis at Politecnico di Milano*, pp. 10.

Itami, H., Nishino, K. (2010). Killing two birds with one stone. Profit for now and learning for the future, *Long Range Planning*, nr 43, 365.

Jabłoński, A. (2008). Modele biznesu w sektorach pojawiających się i schyłkowych. Tworzenie przewagi konkurencyjnej przedsiębiorstwa opartej na jakości i kryteriach ekologicznych, *Wyższa Szkoła Biznesu w Dąbrowie Górniczej*, Dąbrowa Górnicza.

Johnson, M.W. (2013). Rozwój przez innowacje w modelu biznesu, *HBR Polska*, nr 9 (127).

Johnson, M.W., Christensen, C.M., Kagermann, H. (2008). Reinventing your business model, *Harvard Business Review*, nr 86, 2.

Kavussanu, M., Stanger, N. (2017). Moral behavior in sport, *Current Opinion in Psychology*, 16, 185–192. doi: 10.1016/j.copsyc.2017.05.010

Kay, J. 2006. Podstawy sukcesu firmy, *PWE*, Warszawa.

Kim, W.Ch, Mauborgne, R. (2005). *Strategia błękitnego oceanu. Jak stworzyć wolną przestrzeń rynkową i sprawić, by konkurencja stała się nieistotna.* Wydawnictwo MT Biznes, Warszawa.

Kondström, D. (2010). Towards a service-based business model. Key aspects for future competitive advantage, *European Management Journal*, nr 28, 482.

Kotelnikov, V. (2010). Business model. The way of winning the competition battle and creating economic, http://www.1000ventures.com. Accessed date 10.09.2021.

Kotler, Philip (2005) *Marketing*, Wydawnictwo Rebis, Poznań.

Kujala, S., Artto, K., Aaltonen, P., Turkulainen, V. (2010). Business models in project-based firms. Toward a typology of solution-specific business models, *International Journal of Project Management*, nr 28, 96–106.

Lee, M.J., Whitehead, J., Balchin, N. (2000). The measurement of values in youth sport: development of the youth sport values questionnaire, *Journal of Sport & Exercise Psychology*, 22, 307–326.

Lee, M.J., Whitehead, J., Balchin, N. (2013). Which sport values are most important to young people? The measurement of values in youth sport: development of the youth sport values questionnaires. Values in youth sport and physical education, Routledge, 69–85.

Linder J., Cantrell S. (2000). Changing business models. Surveying the landscape, *Accenture Institute for Strategic Change*, Vienna.

Lisein O., Pichault F., Desmech J. (2009). Les business models des societies de service actives dans le secteur Open Source, *Systems d'Information et Management*, 14 (2), 7–38.

Macdonald, E.K., Kleinaltenkamp, M., Wilson, H.N. (2016). How business customers judge solutions: solution quality and value-in-use, *Journal of Marketing*, 80 (3), 96–120. doi:10.1509/jm.15.0109

MacLean, J., Hamm, S. (2008). Values and sport participation: comparing participant groups, age and gender, *Journal of Sport Behavior*, 31 (4) 352.

Magretta, J. (2002). Why business models matter? *Harvard Business Review*, 80 (5), 86–92.

Malone, T.W., Weill, P., Lai, R.K., D'Urso, V.T., Herman, G., Apel, T.G., Woerner, S.L. (2006). Do some business models perform better than others? *MIT Working Paper*, 4615-06.

Maxwell, A., Rankin, S. (2007). *Building a better business model*, CATA Alliance & Technology Marketing Resource Centre, Canada.

Mirabile, R.J. (1996). Translating company values into performance outcomes, *Human Resource Professional*, 9 (4), 25–28.

Mitchell, D., Coles, C. (2003). The ultimate competitive advantage of continuing business model innovation, *The Journal of Business Strategy*, 24, 15–21.

Morris, M., Schindehutte, M., Allen, J. (2004). The entrepreneur's business model. Toward a unified perspective, *Journal of Business Research*, 58, 726–735.

Muszyński, M. (2006). *Aktywne metody prowadzenia strategii przedsiębiorstwa*, Wydawnictwo Placet, Warszawa.

Nam-Ik, K., Sun-Mun, P. (2017). The relationship between media sports involvement experiences and sports values and sports participation, *International Journal of Applied Engineering Research*, 12 (20), 9768–9773.

Nascimento Junior, J.R.A., Morais Freire, G.L., Vila Nova de Moraes, J.F., de Sousa Fortes, L., de Oliveira, D.V., Cronin, L.D. (2021) Does life skills development within sport predict the social behaviours and sports values of youth futsal players? *International Journal of Sport and Exercise Psychology*, 1–15, doi:10.1080/1612197X.2021.1907764

Neely, A., Delbridge, R. (2007). Effective business models. What do they mean for Whitehall, Sunningdale Institute [online], http://www.national-school.gov.uk/sunningdaleinstitute. Last access 10.09.2021.

Nielsen, Ch., Bukh, N. (2008). What constitutes a business model. The perception of financial analysts, *Working Paper Series Department of Business Studies No 4*, Aalborg University, Denmark.

Niemczyk, J. (2010). Modele biznesowe [in:] Morawski, W., Niemczyk, J., Perechuda, K., Stańczyk-Hugiet, E., *Zarządzanie. Kanony i trendy*, Wydawnictwo C.H. Beck, Warszawa.

Nogalski, B. (2009). Modele biznesu jako narzędzie reorientacji strategicznej przedsiębiorstw, *Master of Business Administration*, 2, 3–14.

Obłój, K. (2002). *Tworzywo skutecznych strategii*, PWE, Warszawa.

Osterwalder, A., Pigneur, Y. (2002). An e-business model ontology for modeling e-business, *15th Blend Electronic Commerce Conference e-Reality: Constructing the e-Economy*, Słowenia 17–19 czerwca.

Osterwalder, A., Pigneur, Y. (2010). Business model generation, *John Wiley & Sons Inc.*, New Jersey, USA.

Osterwalder, A., Pigneur, Y., Tucci, C.L. (2005). Clarifying business model. Origins, present and future of the concept, *Communications of the Association for Information Systems*, 16, 1–25

Osterwalder A. *What is a business model?* http://businessmodelalchemist.com/blog/2005/11/ what-is-business-model.html, access: 12.03.2022.

Petri, J., Jacob, F. (2017). Hunting for value: how to enable value-in-use? A conceptual model, *Journal of Creating Value*, 3 (1), 50–62. doi: 10.1177/2394964317694780

Porter, M.E., (1985). *Competitive advantage. Creating and sustaining superior performance,* The Free Press, New York.

Porter, M.E. (2001). Strategy and the Internet, Harvard Business Review on advanced strategy, *Harvard Business School Corporation*, Boston.

Rappa, M.A. (2004). The utility business model and the future of computing service, *IBM Systems Journal*, nr 43.

Rappa, M.A. (2010). Business models on the web, http://digitalenterprise.org/models/models.html, Accessed date: 11.09.2021.

Ratten, V, Thompson, A-J. (2020). Digital sport entrepreneurial ecosystems, *Thunderbird International Business Review* 2020, 1–14. doi: 10.1002/tie.22160

Rokita, J. (2005). *Zarządzanie strategiczne. Tworzenie I utrzymywanie przewagi konkurencyjnej,* Polskie Wydawnictwo Ekonomiczne.

Romanowska, M. (2005). Analiza i planowanie strategiczne w małej firmie. [in:] Zarządzanie strategiczne. Strategie małych firm. *Prace Naukowe Wałbrzyskiej Wyższej Szkoły Zarządzania i Przedsiębiorczości* (pp. 15–30), Wałbrzych.

Sandberg, K.D. (2002). Is it time to trade in your business model? *Harvard Management Update*, pp. 10.

Sarja, Asko (2006). *Predictive and Optimised Life Cycle Management: Buildings and Infrastructure*, Taylor & Francis, London, 2006. pp. 630.

Sceulovs, D., Gaile-Sarkane, E., Kaze, V. (2011). E-environment benefits for Latvian sustainable business development, *Research papers*. ISSN 1822-6760, Management Theory and Studies for Rural Business and Infrastructure Development, nr 2 (26).

Seddon, P.B., Lewis, G.P., Freeman, P., Shanks, G. (2004). The case for viewing business models as abstractions of strategy, *Communications of the Association for Information Systems*, 13, 427–440.

Shafer, S.M., Smith, H.J., Linder, J.C. (2005). The power of business models, *Business Horizons*, 48, 199–207.

Shah, D., Davidi, I., Shapira, Y., Allen, R. (2005). Web 2.0: Hype, Reality or the Future? (accessed: 10.07.2021) http://rallenhome.com/essay

Slywotzky, A., Morrison, D., Andelman, B. (2000). *Strefa zysku*, PWE, Warszawa.

Smith, Adam (1954) *Badanie nad naturą i przyczynami bogactwa narodów*, vol 1., PWE, Warszawa, pp. 81.

Smith, W.K., Binns, A., Tushman, M.L. (2010). Complex business models. Managing strategic paradoxes simultaneously, *Long Range Planning*, 43, 448–461.

Sorescu, A., Frambach, R.T., Singh, J., Rangaswamy, A., Bridges, Ch. (2011). Innovations in retail business models, *Journal of Retailing*, New York University, Elsevier Inc., 1, 3–16.

Teece, D.J. (2010). Business models. Business strategy and innovation, *Long Range Planning*, 43, 172–194.

Timmers, P. (1998). Business models for electronic markets, *Electronic Market*, 8 (2), 3–8.

Tuli, K.R., Kohli, A.K., Bharadwaj, S.G. (2007). Rethinking customer solutions: from product bundles to relational processes, *Journal of Marketing*, 71 (3), 1–17.

Van Wart, Montgomery (1998). *Changing Public Sector Values*, Routledge, New York, pp. 6.

Vankatraman, N., Henderson, J.C. (1998). Real strategies for virtual organizing, *Sloan Management Review*, 40, 33–48.

Vargo, S.L., Lusch, R.F. (2004). The four service marketing myths: remnants of a goods-based, manufacturing model, *Journal of Service Research*, 6 (4), 324–335. doi: 10.1177/1094670503262946.

Vargo, S.L., Lusch, R.F. (2008). Service-dominant logic: Continuing the evolution. *Journal of the Academy of Marketing Science,* 36(1), 1–10. doi: 10.1007/s11747–007–0069–6

Vargo, S.L., Lusch, R.F. (2015). Institutions and axioms: an extension and update of service-dominant logic, *Journal of the Academy of Marketing Science*, 44 (1), 5–23. doi:10.1007/s11747-015-0456-3

Voelpel, S., Leibold, M., Tekie, E., von Krogh, G. (2005). Escaping the red queen effect in competitive strategy. Sense-testing business models, *European Management Journal*, 23, 37–49.

Warner, K.S., Wager, M. (2019). Building dynamic capabilities for digital transformation: an ongoing process of strategic renewal, *Long Range Planning*, 52 (3), 326–349.

Waśkowski, Z., Jasiulewicz, A. (2021). Consumer engagement using digital technologies in the process of co-creating consumer value in the sports market, *Journal of Physical Education and Sport*, 21 (2), 1131–1141.

*Webster's New World Dictionary*. (1978). World Publishing Co., New York.

Weil, P., Vitale, M.R. (2001). *Place to space. Migrating to ebusiness models,* HBR Press, Boston.

Wikström, K., Artto, K., Kujala, J., Söderlund, J. (2010). Business models in project business, *International Journal of Project Management, 28,* 832–841.

Williams, R.M. Jr. (1979). Change and stability in values systems: a sociological perspective, [in] Rokeach, M. (eds) *Understanding Human Values*, The Free Press, New York, NY, pp. 15–46.

Wiśniewski, A. (2021). *Model biznesu klubu piłki siatkowej. W drodze do zwiększania konkurencyjności,* Wydawnictwo Uniwersytetu Warmińsko-Mazurskiego w Olsztynie, Olsztyn town.

Witt de, B., Meyer, R. (2007). *Synteza strategii. Tworzenie przewagi konkurencyjnej przez tworzenie paradoksów,* Polskie Wydawnictwo Ekonomiczne, Warszawa.

Yip, G.S. (2004). Using strategy to change your business model, *Business Strategy Review, Polskie Wydawnictwo Ekonomiczne* (15, pp. 17–24). http://businessmodelalchemist.com/blog/2005/11/what-is-business-model.html; http://www.boardofinnovation.com/howbuildanybusinessmodelwithonly10blocks Published on 19th March 2009

# 2 Business Models in Sports Organizations and Sport-Related Service Industries

## Mapping the Research Field

*Andrzej Lis*

## Introduction

The concept of a business model, which reflects a company's strategy (Casadesus-Masanell & Ricart, 2010), is one of the topics attracting a lot of attention among researchers examining the ways in which companies operate (Zott et al., 2011). Although there is a lack of observable consensus in defining a business model, the gist of the concept is accurately explained by Teece (2010, p. 172), who states that

> [w]henever a business enterprise is established, it either explicitly or implicitly employs a particular business model that describes the design or architecture of the value creation, delivery, and capture mechanisms it employs. The essence of a business model is in defining the manner by which the enterprise delivers value to customers, entices customers to pay for value, and converts those payments to profit.

According to Casadesus-Masanell and Ricart (2011), a business model consists of policy, asset and governance choices leading to 'flexible' (changing quickly) or 'rigid' (stable over time) consequences. The business model framework proposed by Johnson et al. (2008) includes the four following components: a 'customer value proposition', a 'profit formula', 'key resources' and 'key processes'.

The interest of scholars in examining business models translates into growing research production and accumulated research output. As of 16 August 2021, nearly 35,500 publications containing the phrase 'business model' in their titles, keywords and abstracts (topic search) were retrieved from the Scopus database. Nevertheless, the issue of business models in sports organizations seems to be a relatively unexplored field. A topic search for the logical conjunction of

DOI: 10.4324/9781003270126-3

expressions 'business model' and 'sport' in publications indexed by Scopus resulted in only 182 items. What is more, the research field has not been mapped or profiled, so far. As mapping the structure of a research field seems to be a valuable contribution, which provides scholars cultivating the field with a clear picture of the status quo and potential avenues for further inquiry, the lack of such a study in regard to business models in sports organizations may be considered a gap in the body of knowledge.

In order to contribute to the development of the field and fill the identified gap, the aim of this study is to explore and map research on business models in sports organizations and sport-related service industries. The research process is focused on the following study questions: (1) What is productivity in the field and what are the key contributors to research output?, (2) What are the core references in research on business models in sports organizations and sport-related service industries?, (3) What does the conceptual structure of the research field look like? (4) What are the research fronts in the field? The study employs a combination of bibliometric methods (research profiling, citation analysis, co-word analysis, bibliographic coupling) and systematic literature review. The remainder of the chapter consists of five sections. First, the sampling process and research methods are explained. Second, productivity in research on business models in sports organizations and sport-related service industries is analyzed and key contributors are profiled. Third, core references are identified through direct citation analysis. Fourth, the conceptual structure of the field is visualized with the use of co-word analysis. Finally, the research fronts in the field are identified and explored with bibliographic coupling and systematic literature review.

## Materials and methods

### Research sample

The Scopus database was used as a source of bibliometric data for analysis. Along with Web of Science, Scopus is listed among the largest and most reliable databases of quality research publications (Aghaei Chadegani et al., 2013; Schotten et al., 2017; Zhu & Liu, 2020). As the study combines bibliometric methods with systematic literature review, the sampling process followed the model typical of the latter method, recommended by Moher et al. (2009), and consisted of three steps (Figure 2.1).

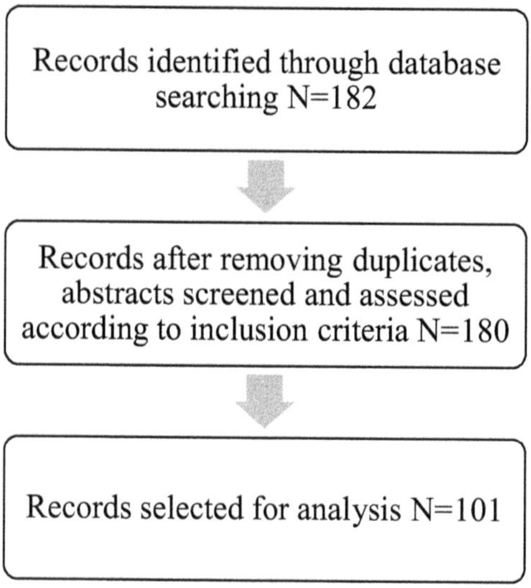

> Records identified through database searching N=182

⬇

> Records after removing duplicates, abstracts screened and assessed according to inclusion criteria N=180

⬇

> Records selected for analysis N=101

*Figure 2.1* Research sampling process.

First, as of 16 August 2021, a search was conducted in Scopus for publications with a conjunction of the terms 'business model' and 'sport' in their titles, keywords and abstracts (topic search). 182 items were retrieved. Second, duplicates (two items) were removed. In the third stage, the abstracts of the remaining 180 publications were screened and assessed in accordance with the following inclusion/exclusion criteria: (1) only publications referring to the construct of a business model or its components (i.e. customer value proposition, profit formula, key resources, and/or key processes) in the context of sport were included, (2) publications referring to business models of sports organizations (e.g. sports clubs, associations, leagues, federations) were included; (3) publications referring to business models of sport-related services e.g. eSports, sports tourism, sports betting/wagering and sports broadcasting industries were included, provided that their contents were significantly related to sport; (4) publications referring to business models of companies manufacturing and/or trading sports goods (e.g. sports clothes or footwear, sports nutrients) were excluded. As a result of this procedure, 79 items were excluded and 101 publications were selected for analysis.

The publications comprising the sample are distributed over 17 non-exclusive subject areas defined by Scopus. The most numerous among them are Social Sciences (42 items) and Business, Management

*Table 2.1* Parameters of the research sample

| Category | Items (N) |
|---|---|
| Subject area | Social Sciences (42); Business, Management and Accounting (40); Computer Science (17); Economics, Econometrics and Finance (12); Environmental Science (12); Energy (11); Engineering (11); Health Professions (11); Medicine (11); Psychology (6); Decision Sciences (5); Mathematics (3); Arts and Humanities (1), Earth and Planetary Sciences (1); Material Science (1); Multidisciplinary (1); Physics and Astronomy (1) |
| Document type | Article (74); Conference Paper (16); Book Chapter (8); Review (2); Book (1) |
| Language | English (95); Spanish (5); French (1) |

Source: Own study based on data retrieved from Scopus (16 August 2021).

and Accounting (40). Articles (74) represent the most common type of documents. English (95) is found to be the dominant language of publication. Detailed parameters of the sample are provided in Table 2.1.

***Methods and instruments***

The methodology toolbox combined bibliometric methods with systematic literature review. The study employed the method of research profiling (Porter et al., 2002) and one of its components, i.e. general publication profiling, in order to identify leading contributors to research on business models in sports organizations and sport-related service industries. The focus was on research productivity and the most productive countries, research institutions and source titles. Citation analysis, representing science mapping methods (Zupic & Čater, 2015), was used to identify core references in the field. Another science mapping method, i.e. co-word analysis (Callon et al., 1983, 1991; He, 1999) served for recognition of the conceptual structure of the field. For this purpose an analysis of high-frequency keywords was conducted. Bibliographic coupling (Kessler, 1963) contributed to identifying research fronts. Last but not least, identified research fronts were explored using systematic literature review (Booth et al., 2012; Czakon, 2011; Mazur & Orłowska, 2018; Tranfield et al., 2003). Science mapping analyses were supported by VOSviewer software (van Eck & Waltman, 2010, 2020). The detailed parameters of VOSviewer employed for analysis are presented in Table 2.2.

*Table 2.2* VOSviewer parameters used for analysis

| Type of analysis | Citation analysis | Co-word (keywords co-occurrence) analysis | Bibliographic coupling |
|---|---|---|---|
| Unit of analysis | Documents | All keywords | Documents |
| Counting method | Full counting | Full counting | Full counting |
| Method of normalization of strength of the links between items | Association strength method | Association strength method | Association strength method |
| Layout | | | |
| Attraction | 2 (default value) | 2 (default value) | 2 (default value) |
| Repulsion | 0 (default value) | 0 (default value) | 1 (default value) |
| Clustering | | | |
| Resolution parameter (detail of clustering) | 1 (default value) | 1 (default value) | 1 (default value) |
| Minimum cluster size [$N$] | 10 | 5 | 1 |
| Merging small clusters | Switched on | Switched on | Switched on |
| High-frequency keywords used for analysis [$N$] | NA | 33 | NA |
| The largest set of connected documents used for analysis [$N$] | NA | NA | 71 |
| Minimum occurrences of a keyword/ minimum number of citations of a document to be included for analysis [$N$] | 0 | 3 | 0 |

Source: Own study based on VOSviewer parameters (16 August 2021).

## Results

### Research productivity

Research productivity within the field was measured with the attributes of the number of publications per annum and the number of citations received per annum (Figure 2.2). The 101 publications comprising the research sample were published between 2004 and 2021, which represents an annual average production at the level of 5.61 publications. The total number of citations received by the publications under analysis over the same period equals 742, which translates into 41.2 citations per annum and 7.34 citations per publication. Nevertheless, significant differences in the yearly distribution of research production are observable. Between 2004 and 2012, there were only weak signals of research interest in the issue of business models in sports and sport-related service industries, marked by single publications and citations. The period 2013 to 2019 may be labeled as the start-up or emergence period, when the yearly research production experienced ups and down (fluctuating from 2 to 12 items) and the number of citations grew steadily from 22 to 89. The last two years (2020–2021) may be considered as manifesting the shift to the growth stage in the research field lifecycle as both the number of publications and the number of citations increased significantly.

The leading contributors to research production in the field are scholars from the United Kingdom (18 publications), Spain (17), the United States (15), Germany (10), China (9), and Croatia (9). The top most productive research institutions include: Rijeka University, Croatia (8 publications), the University of Castilla-La Mancha, Spain (4), the University of Sevilla, Spain (4), and Nottingham Trent University, the United Kingdom (3). The source titles of primary choice among the researchers in the field are: *Sustainability Switzerland*

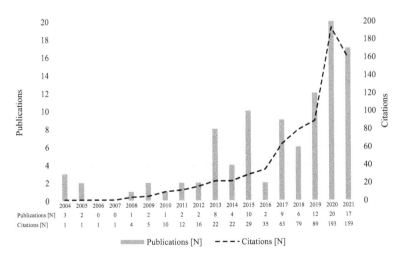

*Figure 2.2* Productivity in research on business models in sports organizations and sport-related service industries.
Source: Own study based on data retrieved from Scopus (16 August 2021).

(6 publications), *Sport, Business and Management: An International Journal* (5), *European Sport Management Quarterly* (3), *Journal of Physical Education and Sport* (3), *Managing Sport and Leisure* (3), and *Soccer and Society* (3).

## Core references

The number of citations received may be considered as a measure of the influence of a publication in a research field. It is based on the assumption that publications recognized by the members of a community are cited more often than others. Thus, citation analysis is a useful tool to identify influential core references. The bias toward earlier publications is an inherent weakness of the method in analyses conducted with the use of VOSviewer, but it can be mitigated through employment of the attribute of the normalized number of citations (i.e. "the number of citations of the document divided by the average number of citations of all documents published in the same year and included in the data that is provided to VOSviewer"; van Eck & Waltman, 2020, p. 37). The visualization of the findings from citation analysis for research on business models in sports organizations and sport-related service industries is presented in Figure 2.3. In the map showing item density, colors ranging from blue through green and yellow to red correspond to the increasing number of citations (or normalized citations) received by the analyzed items. Moreover, the prominence of the publications is marked by font size.

The outcomes of citation analysis indicate the following core references: García-Fernández et al. (2018) (80 citations), Aversa et al. (2015) (74), Yeh and Taylor (2008) (37), McNamara et al. (2013) (35), Wemmer et al. (2016) (32), Hutchins et al. (2009) (31). Taking into account the normalized number of citations, publications worth noticing are the studies by: Ratten (2020) (7.19), Crick and Crick (2020) (6.38), Aversa et al. (2015) (5.03), García-Fernández et al. (2018) (4.80), and Scholz (2019) (4.14).

## Conceptual structure of the field

The conceptual structure of research on business models in sports and sport-related service industries was identified with the use of co-word (keywords co-occurrence) analysis. Co-word analysis (Callon et al., 1983) is

a content analysis technique that uses the words in documents to establish relationships and build conceptual structure of the

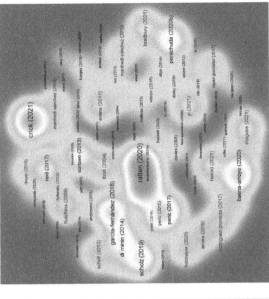
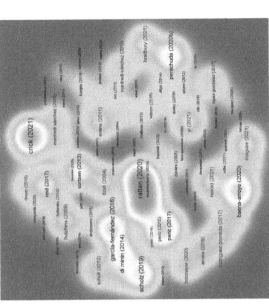

*Figure 2.3* Item density visualization of citation analysis of research on business models in sports organizations and sport-related service industries.

Source: Own study based on data retrieved from Scopus and analyzed with VOSviewer (16 August 2021).

domain. The idea underlying the method is that, when words frequently co-occur in documents, it means that the concepts behind those words are closely related. (...) The output of co-word analysis is a network of themes and their relations that represent the conceptual space of a field. The semantic map helps to understand its cognitive structure (Börner et al., 2003).

(Zupic and Čater, 2015, p. 435)

In the network map of the research field, visualized with the use of VOSviewer, the distance between two items corresponds to relatedness between them, i.e. the closer two keywords are located to each other, the stronger is the relatedness observed.

The publications comprising the sample provide 607 keywords, of which 512 occurred only once. The most frequently occurring keywords are: 'sports' (18), 'sport' (15), 'business model' (12), 'business modeling' (10), 'business models' (9), 'COVID-19' (6). Following the formula provided by Donohue (1974; as cited in Guo et al., 2017), the minimum number of high-frequency keywords to be taken for analysis equals 32, which corresponds to keywords of a minimum three occurrences. Among 34 such keywords, the one related to the study process ('questionnaire survey') was excluded, so finally 33 items were subject to co-word (keywords co-occurrence) analysis. The network visualization of the outcomes of analysis is presented in Figure 2.4 and the detailed composition of thematic clusters representing the conceptual structure of the field in Table 2.3.

The analysis indicates four thematic clusters in research on business models in sports organizations and sport-related service industries. Cluster 1 (marked in red in Figure 2.4) encompasses various aspects of sport management, including entrepreneurship, marketing, human resources management aimed at customers' satisfaction, and organizations' efficiency and performance. Cluster 2 (green) establishes a bridge between business models in sports and those in sport-related service industries such as sports tourism or sports journalism. Cluster 3 (blue) focuses on business models and financial performance in sport. Cluster 4 (yellow) highlights the issues of business model innovations and new business models in sport.

### Research fronts

Research fronts in studies on business models in sports organizations and sport-related service industries were discovered by the use of the bibliographic coupling method (Figure 2.5). As noted by Zupic and Čater (2015, p. 439),

*Figure 2.4* Network visualization of co-word analysis of research on business models in sports and sport-related service industries.

Source: Own study based on data retrieved from Scopus and analyzed with VOSviewer (16 August 2021).

*Table 2.3* Composition of thematic clusters in research on business models in sports and sport-related service industries (co-word analysis)

| Cluster label | Color | N | Items |
| --- | --- | --- | --- |
| Sport management | Red | 13 | Commerce, COVID-19, efficiency, entrepreneurship, football, human, management, marketing, performance, satisfaction, Spain, sport management, television |
| Business models in sport-related services | Green | 8 | Business development, business models, digital journalism, innovation, sport tourism, sports journalism, sports management, sustainability |

*(Continued)*

| Cluster label | Color | N | Items |
|---|---|---|---|
| Business models and financial performance in sport | Blue | 7 | Business, business models, business modeling, finance, model, sport, tourism |
| Business model innovation in sport | Yellow | 5 | Business model innovation, competition, governance, new business models, sports |

Source: Own study based on data retrieved from Scopus and analyzed with VOSviewer (16 August 2021).

[t]he concept of research front was introduced by Price (1965) and is used to describe current scientific papers that cite the publications in the knowledge base. At any given time, these papers are recently published papers that represent the state of the art of a scientific field. Examining the research front of topic or research field is a task particularly suitable for bibliographic coupling since this method uses reference lists for coupling and does not require the documents to be cited in order to connect them.

In bibliographic coupling, the more often references are cited by two publications under analysis, the higher is the reported level of similarity between them. In the network visualization produced with the use of VOSviewer, the spatial proximity between the items corresponds to their relatedness. Due to technical limitations of the visualization functionalities of VOSviewer, the map does not show all the items included in the identified clusters. Therefore, the detailed composition of clusters will be described in the following paragraphs.

Cluster 1 (marked in green in Figure 2.5) combines research on business models in sports clubs and other sports organizations (e.g. leagues, associations, tennis tournament organizers). The studies are focused on configuration and types of business models, financial performance, and relationships with sports stakeholders (investors and sponsors in particular). Football is found to be the most popular sport under investigation. Other sports attracting the attention of researchers are volleyball, rugby, tennis and motor racing. Also included are two publications on sports journalism. Cluster 2 (red) is oriented to the business models of amateur/non-profit sports clubs, fitness centers and sports facilities. Business models of sports organizations in the COVID-19 context constitute another stream of research. There are as well single publications related to sports tourism and electronic sports. Research categorized under the umbrella of Cluster 3 (blue) is concentrated on business models of sports media and betting companies. Cluster 4 (yellow) deals with business models

*Figure 2.5* Network visualization of bibliographic coupling of research on business models in sports organizations and sport-related service industries.

Source: Own study based on data retrieved from Scopus and analyzed with VOSviewer (16 August 2021).

*Table 2.4* Composition of thematic clusters in research on business models in sports and sport-related service industries (bibliographic coupling)

| Research fronts | Clusters | | | | | |
|---|---|---|---|---|---|---|
| | *Green (N = 19)* | *Red (N = 19)* | *Blue (N = 11)* | *Yellow (N = 9)* | *Violet (N = 7)* | *Light blue (N = 6)* |
| Business models of football clubs | Bennike et al. (2020); Di Minin et al. (2014); Rodriguez-Pomeda et al. (2017) | McNamara et al. (2013); Prado-Román et al. (2019) | | | Amara et al. (2005) | |
| Financial performance of football clubs' business models | Di Simone and Zanardi (2020); Holzmayer and Schmidt (2020); Litvishko et al. (2019); Perechuda (2020a); Perechuda (2020b); Quansah et al. (2021) | | | | | |
| Business models in sports other than football | Abere et al. (2012); Aversa et al. (2015); Maltese and Veran (2013); Wilson et al. (2015); Wiśniewski (2021) | | | | | |
| Relationships with investors and sponsors | Dilys and Gargasas (2014); Huth (2020); Pittz et al. (2020) | | | | | |

(*Continued*)

| | | | |
|---|---|---|---|
| Business models of amateur-/non-profit sports clubs | | Bradbury et al. (2021); Crick and Crick (2020); Escamilla-Fajardo, Parra-Camacho, et al. (2021); Reid (2017); Wemmer et al. (2016) | |
| Business models of sports organizations in the COVID-19 context | Quansah et al. (2021) | Escamilla-Fajardo, Alguacil, et al. (2021); Escamilla-Fajardo, Parra-Camacho, et al. (2021); Ratten (2020) | Herold et al. (2021) |
| Business models of fitness centers | | Baena-Arroyo et al. (2020); García-Fernández et al. (2018); León-Quismondo et al. (2020a); León-Quismondo et al. (2020b); Yi et al. (2021) | |
| Business models of sports facilities | Caldas et al. (2020) | Ramchandani et al. (2018); Santacruz Lozano et al. (2021) | |

Clusters

| Research fronts | Green (N = 19) | Red (N = 19) | Blue (N = 11) | Yellow (N = 9) | Violet (N = 7) | Light blue (N = 6) |
|---|---|---|---|---|---|---|
| Sports tourism | | Wise et al. (2019); Yu et al. (2021) | | Jenkins and Rios-Morales (2013); Perić and Wise (2015); Perić et al. (2016); Perić et al. (2017); Perić et al. (2018); Perić and Slavić (2019); Perić, Vitezić, and Durkin Badurina (2019); Perić, Vitezić, and Mekinc (2019); Waśkowski and Jasiulewicz (2021) | | |
| Business models in sports media and betting companies | Manfredi Sánchez et al. (2015a); Manfredi Sánchez et al. (2015b) | | Bonaut-Iriarte and Vicent (2020); Borges (2019); Boyle (2015); Buzzelli et al. (2020); Evens et al. (2011); Fortunato (2013); Maxcy (2013); Martin-Guart et al. (2017); López-González et al. (2017) | | | |

| Sports organizations' branding and their relationships with fans | | Cortsen (2013); Cortsen (2017); Herold et al. (2021); Hutchins et al. (2009); Scholl and Carlson (2012) |
| Governance and value creation in sports organizations | | Amara et al. (2005) |
| | | Bayle (2021); Jacopin et al. (2013); Yeh and Taylor (2008) Felczak (2020); Scholz (2019); Vera and Terron (2019) |
| Business models of electronic sports | Dwyer et al. (2019) | |

Source: Own study based on data retrieved from Scopus and analyzed with VOSviewer (16 August 2021).

of sports tourism. Cluster 5 (violet) encompasses research on sports organizations' branding and their relationships with fans. Cluster 6 (light blue) combines studies on governance and value creation in sports organizations as well as business models of electronic sports. Distribution of publications categorized within the bibliographic coupling clusters across the identified research fronts is presented in Table 2.4.

## Discussion

### *Business models of football clubs*

Football is the sport attracting most attention from researchers of business models in sports organizations. Among the studies focused on business models in football, categorized within the green cluster, Bennike et al. (2020) explore the profiles of Danish football clubs and find "the creation of a certain business model of professional Danish football" among the features of these sports organizations. Rodriguez-Pomeda et al. (2017) analyze the case study of the business model of Real Madrid in the context of the experience economy. They recommend, as good practice for other football clubs, developing business models based on enhancing the emotions and commitment of fans. Di Minin et al. (2014) investigate the antecedents of the successful business model of Udinese Calcio, an Italian football club and its attempts to balance sports and financial performance. The club

> in the last twenty years has adopted a business model based on strong investments and quick turnaround of young and promising players, which has turned it into a factory of talents. Udinese Calcio has been able to do so keeping its books in order and at the same time managing excellent results in a very competitive national soccer tournament such as the Italian Serie A.
>
> (Di Minin et al., 2014, p. 319)

The research front focused on business models in football is complemented with three publications included in red and violet clusters. In their study of business models of English football clubs, McNamara et al. (2013) "show that alternative models – based on the acquisition of talent on one dimension and the internal development of shared team experience on the other – lead to differing value creation and value capture outcomes" (McNamara et al., 2013, p. 475). Taking into account the challenges faced by sports clubs due to declining audience, Prado-Román et al. (2019) make an attempt to identify the antecedents of supporters' loyalty focusing on the reputation of football teams and the satisfaction of fans. It may be assumed that the study of Prado-Román et al. (2019) is included in the red cluster due to its links with other publications focused on the issue of loyalty (García-Fernández et al., 2018). Amara et al. (2005) analyze case studies of football clubs in five countries (Algeria, China, England, France, and Japan) in order to explore their business models, which are customized to and under influence of local conditions.

### *Financial performance of football clubs' business models*

The next stream of publications focuses on financial performance of business models. Within this stream, Di Simone and Zanardi (2020) conduct a statistical analysis of the relationships between sports success and financial performance of football clubs. Their study confirms that

> there is stable and significant relationship between the two types of performance and that when detectable this is linked in a positive way to the profit maximization of the business model, suggesting that it is more useful for investor remuneration and to increase technical-tactical resources and therefore sports results.
>
> (Di Simone and Zanardi, 2020, p. 812)

In their statistical analysis of data from the English Premier League, Quansah et al. (2021) explore the importance of various sources of revenues for football clubs and make predictions about the decrease in the level of salaries and transfers due to the lockdown caused by the COVID-19 pandemic. Litvishko et al. (2019) analyze English and Danish football clubs in search of an effective business model. In their opinion,

> one of the ways to optimize the financial stability of professional sports entities can be the implementation of measures to increase the share of tangible assets in the overall structure of non-current capital through the construction of a developed sports infrastructure, as well as diversification of activities via development of related and non-core areas, which will generate income in addition to participation of clubs in sports competitions, due to the synergistic effect of commercial activities under a brand of well-known sports teams, making the parent organization less dependent on the sports component, which will ultimately increase the investment potential of the football industry as a possible area for investing private capital.
>
> (Litvishko et al., 2019, p. 105)

The issue of diversification is also considered by Holzmayer and Schmidt (2020), who investigate the financial performance of diversification strategies in professional football clubs of the English Premier League. Their study indicates the advantage of related diversification over unrelated diversification and a niche strategy (for increasing related diversification) in regard to revenues and profitability. Perechuda (2020b) implements a statistical analysis of financial data of European football clubs to identify the antecedents of their intellectual capital. Salary ratio and leverage ratio are found to be the key factors influencing the added value intellectual coefficient in football organizations. In his second study, Perechuda (2020a) explores the cases of Polish football clubs to assess the usefulness of financial information for managing business models of these organizations. Nevertheless, Perechuda finds that, due to the Polish football clubs' orientation mainly toward social benefits (at the expense of profits), the utility of financial information is rather limited.

### Business models in sports other than football

Besides football, other sports attracting the attention of scholars interested in business models of sports organizations include: volleyball, rugby, tennis and motor racing. For instance, Wiśniewski (2021) analyzes the cases of business models of two volleyball clubs (from Poland and Sweden) and proposes a profile of a volleyball club business model. Wilson et al. (2015) tell the story of the rugby superleague in the United Kingdom regarding its financial situations as well as attendance and participation. Due to its impermanence, a change in the business model of the organization is recommended. Maltese and Veran (2013) analyze the cases of Roland Garros, BNP Paribas Masters and Open 13 in order to compare their business models. Their study, embedded in the resource-based view (RBV) of strategy, emphasizes the importance of deployment and control of organizations' resources. Abere et al. (2012) explore the business model of the National Association for Stock Car Auto Racing (NASCAR), the largest car racing organization in the United States, and the key antecedents of its success. Aversa et al. (2015) compare and contrast the business models of high and low performance F1 racing firms. They discover that "configurations of two business models – one focused on selling technology to competitors, the other one on developing and trading human resources with competitors – are associated with high performance" (Aversa et al., 2015, p. 655).

## Relationships with investors and sponsors

Relationships with stakeholders, investors and sponsors in particular, are another stream of research. On the one hand, in the context of the United States, return on investments in sports is highlighted as an issue of paramount importance. Thus, Pittz et al. (2020) analyze various business models of sports organizations in order to develop recommendations for optimizing value for stakeholders. On the other hand, Huth (2020), who employs a questionnaire survey to identify the motivations for investors to purchase financial instruments of European football clubs, indicates that emotion-related aspects dominate rather than any expectation of financial returns. Dilys and Gargasas (2014) develop a structural business model of cooperation between sports organizations and sports sponsors. The model combines such components as a sports product, image, values, and association in order to create attractiveness for audience and sponsors.

## Business models of amateur/ non-profit clubs

The business models of amateur/ non-profit clubs are another interesting stream of research. This issue is studied in various national contexts (e.g. New Zealand, Germany, Spain). Bradbury et al. (2021) analyze the business models of amateur sports clubs in New Zealand and recommend forming partnerships in order to increase membership and improve the management and the financial situation of clubs. Crick and Crick (2020) study coopetition strategies among small sports clubs in New Zealand and confirm that coopetition has a positive effect on sales performance. Nevertheless, it is extremely important that clubs focus on engaging in relationships with trustworthy partners in order to avoid the risk of being outcompeted by them. Similarly, Wemmer et al. (2016), in their questionnaire study conducted among German non-profit sports clubs, show that engagement in coopetition has positive effects on organizational performance because of the access it offers to external knowledge and the implementation of innovative organizational solutions. Reid (2017) studies the case of a football social enterprise to discuss the issue of business models of social enterprises operating local voluntary sports clubs, which can be considered as an example of business model innovation. The study identifies key success factors and challenges faced by such organizations. Escamilla-Fajardo, Parra-Camacho, et al. (2021) investigate the entrepreneurial orientation of Spanish non-profit clubs as a response to management challenges during recession in the context of the COVID-19 pandemic. They observe differences in adaptation ability, financial and service performance and the perceived level of service quality in connection to clubs' attitudes to entrepreneurship.

## Business models of sports organizations in the COVID-19 context

As the COVID-19 pandemic and related social distancing limitations have significantly influenced the operations of sports organizations, investigating the resilience of their business models is among the most important themes in recent studies. For instance, Ratten (2020) reviews existing research in order to elicit recommendations for adjustments to business models that allow sports companies to respond to the challenges of the COVID-19 pandemic. These adjustments are focused on sports entrepreneurship and entrepreneurial thinking to deal with the uncertainty of the environment. Escamilla-Fajardo, Parra-Camacho et al. (2021) investigate the entrepreneurial orientation of Spanish non-profit clubs as a response to management challenges during recession in the context of the COVID-19 pandemic. They observe differences in adaptation ability, financial and service performance and the perceived level of service quality in connection to clubs' attitudes to entrepreneurship. Escamilla-Fajardo, Alguacil, et al. (2021) analyze adaptation of Spanish sports clubs in the context of the COVID-19 pandemic challenges in regard to social performance. The aim of the study is "to find what perceptions of the environment can influence the BMA [(business model adaptation)], and to investigate what influence [it] has on the social performance of this type of entity" (Escamilla-Fajardo, Alguacil et al., 2021, p. 1). The COVID-19 context is also included in the aforementioned study by Quansah et al. (2021), who explore the importance of various sources of revenues for football clubs in the English Premier League and make predictions about a decrease in the level of salaries and transfers due to the lockdown triggered by the COVID-19 pandemic. Herold et al. (2021) investigate the impact of the absence of in-stadium spectators, due to COVID-19 restrictions, on the emotions of TV viewers and their engagement with sponsors.

## Business models of fitness centers

The next line of research on business models is focused on fitness centers. The questionnaire-based study by Baena-Arroyo et al. (2020) compares and contrasts the service experience and satisfaction of customers attending traditional instructor-led and virtual fitness classes. The questionnaire survey by García-Fernández et al. (2018) makes an attempt to understand the relationship among perceived quality and service convenience on perceived value, satisfaction, and client loyalty in low-cost fitness centers. […] Findings demonstrate the importance of proper management of non-monetary sacrifices and perceived quality by the managers of these sport organizations, since client loyalty could depend on factors of these emerging sport models.

(García-Fernández et al., 2018, p. 250)

León-Quismondo et al. (2020b) search for best practices in the business models of fitness centers in Spain in regard to "customer service, offered service, marketing, facilities, and general terms and conditions". Their study finds that "[k]ind customer service, the existence of loyalty programs, enough tangible quality, and online marketing strategies are essential for fitness centers' success" (León-Quismondo et al., 2020b, p. 1). In another questionnaire-based study, León-Quismondo et al. (2020a) highlight the following key success factors "[c]leanliness and hygiene, kindness in customer service, closeness to member homes and days and hours of operation" (León-Quismondo et al., 2020a, p. 233). In their quantitative study, Yi et al. (2021) analyze visit frequency in South Korean fitness centers as a factor influencing the commitment and retention of customers.

### *Business models of sports facilities*

The management of sports facilities and their business models are another stream of research in the field. Ramchandani et al. (2018) study performance and the changes in business models of public sports facilities in the United Kingdom as a result of reduction in public subsidies. Their study shows an increase in financial performance as a result of growing quality and higher charges, but this is achieved at the expense of social inclusion. Santacruz Lozano et al. (2021) analyze differences in the management of sports facilities in Spain relating to the form of ownership (public or private) and the type of a business model. The study indicates "significant differences for most of the variables analyzed (surface area, number of users, income from quotas, extraordinary income, total income, monthly income per customer and average monthly quota) between public and private sports facilities and between business models" (Santacruz Lozano et al., 2021, p. 38). Caldas et al. (2020) develop a model of a multisided digital platform connecting owners of sports facilities, their customers and platform administrators. Such a platform may be considered as a factor driving business model innovation in the market and as a manifestation of digitalization processes in sport-related industries.

## Business models in sports tourism

Business models are an interesting element of the research agenda in sports tourism. Research production dealing with business models in the context of sports tourism is dominated by a team of researchers grouped around Marko Perić from the University of Rijeka in Croatia. Perić et al. (2017) identify gaps and provide recommendations for future research in sports tourism. Their study "addresses types of sport experiences, economic dimensions of experiences and business models to determine capabilities of delivering different types of experiences" (Perić et al., 2017, p. 58). Perić et al. (2016) develop a business model for sustainable sports tourism aimed at delivering unique added value to customers, combining 'experience oriented' tourism and 'performance oriented' sport. Their framework may be considered as a useful tool for business practitioners, and small sports tourism businesses in particular. In one of their subsequent works Perić et al. (2018) study the natural environment and sports safety and security as components of business models in sports tourism that are important in providing an experience to customers. Combining the experience of sports tourism customers and event organizers, Perić, Vitezić, and Đurkin Badurina (2019) propose three business models customized to the needs of various segments of outdoor sports tourists, labeling them as 'moderate recreationists', 'nature lovers' and 'enthusiasts'. The quantitative study by Yu et al. (2021) confirms that the satisfaction gained from sports events has positive effects for both sponsors and the tourism attractiveness of a the place where an event is held.

The issue of business models in the context of sports tourism is often explored with the use of the case study methodology. For instance, Perić and Wise (2015) analyze the two cases of Croatian companies operating in the sports tourism industry in order to compare and contrast experiences provided to their customers. Their findings show that "despite different approaches, both companies provide [...] tourists with similar tennis experiences, and that some of other variables, primarily features of a sports facility ([...] tennis courts) affect the type of an experience" (Perić & Wise, 2015, p. 1000). Perić, Vitezić, and Mekinc (2019) compare and contrast the cases of business models of two (Italian and Croatian) cycling tourism events. "The findings indicate that although the BMs of the two events differ in many aspects, they have a strong emphasis on networks and managerial processes aimed at ensuring participant safety and preservation of the environment" (Perić, Vitezić, & Mekinc,

2019, p. 379). Another multiple case study analysis of business models in sports tourism, with the emphasis on trail running, is provided by Perić and Slavić (2019). The collection of case studies is complemented by the work of Jenkins and Rios-Morales (2013), Waśkowski and Jasiulewicz (2021), and Wise et al. (2019). Jenkins and Rios-Morales (2013) investigate the perceived economic impact of the BRITS week in Laax, Switzerland based on niche snow sports. Waśkowski and Jasiulewicz (2021) analyze engagement of PKO Białystok Half Marathon customers in co-creating value to validate the modified model of the process of absorbing experiences. Their study emphasizes the role of information and communication technologies (ICTs) for co-creation of value for customers. Wise et al. (2019) conduct a benchmarking analysis of sports tourism in Slovenian Pokljuka and develop lessons for Croatian Gorski Kotar. Their study is focused on three aspects, i.e. infrastructure, operations of business and engagement of stakeholders.

### *Business models in sports media and betting companies*

Publications related to business models in sports media and betting companies constitute another research front. Within this front the following streams may be identified: sports journalism, sports transmissions and copyrights, and changes due to digitalization processes. Manfredi Sánchez and associates explore the issue of sports journalism in Spain. In the first of two studies, the authors analyze the value propositions and storytelling approaches of sports journalism businesses (Manfredi Sánchez et al., 2015a). The second study focuses on the two types of projects, i.e. 'hyper-local start-ups' and 'niche information products' in the Spanish sports journalism industry (Manfredi Sánchez et al., 2015b). Buzzelli et al. (2020) analyze the case of The Athletic, i.e. the pay website providing national and local sports news in the United States and the United Kingdom. The business model of The Athletic is identified as a major innovation in the sports media market.

Bonaut-Iriarte and Vicent (2020) explore the case of the business model of the first pay TV in Spain, i.e. Canal Plus, the success of which was founded on sports transmissions. Martín-Guart et al. (2017) discuss the role of sports content, in particular that of football, as an element of value proposition to mitigate the consequences of audience fragmentation in the Spanish TV market. Borges (2019) employs the case study methodology to discuss Portuguese Benfica TV and French PSG TV as examples of the diversification of sports clubs into the media industry. The analysis is focused on the motivations for establishing a media business owned by sports clubs. Boyle (2015) discusses the issue of copyright and its importance for the business models of football associations holding these rights and media broadcasters. Fortunato (2013) analyzes the importance of TV broadcasting rights fees for the revenues of sports organizations, including sports leagues and the International Olympic Committee.

Maxcy (2013) discusses the shifts in sports media as a consequence of the development of digital technologies, including the impact on business models of media companies and sports organizations. López-González et al. (2017) analyze analog and digital sports broadcasting and consider the potential influence of digital technologies on the business models of players in the industry. Evens et al. (2011) focus on "the strategic importance of content in the development of sustainable business models for mobile broadcasting services and [...] discuss the implications of bundling strategies for the viability of these emerging platforms" (Evens et al., 2011, p. 32). Casadesus-Masanell and Campbell (2019) analyze business models and the rivalry between two multi-sided platforms, i.e. Betfair and Flutter, and traditional competitors in the UK sports betting industry.

### Sports organizations' branding and their relationships with fans

Cortsen (2013) explores the case of the ANNIKA BRAND based on sports success in golf. Cortsen (2017) studies approaches to enhancing the branding of female football in Denmark and achieving commercial objectives. As already mentioned, Herold et al. (2021) investigate the consequences of the absence of in-stadium spectators, due to COVID-19 restrictions, on the emotions of TV viewers and their attention to sponsors. Recognizing the paramount importance of websites to connect sports clubs with their fans, Scholl and Carlson (2012) compare the websites of European and North American clubs employing the information management perspective. Hutchins et al. (2009) study the case of MyFootballClub, which "is a popular computer game, Web site, online networking experiment, business model, and an actual soccer club", in order to "show how the professionalization and mediatization of sport has created a longing to reconstruct a kind of communhas around supporter participation in the ownership and running of their team" (Hutchins et al., 2009, p. 89).

### Governance and value creation in sports organizations

Amara et al. (2005) analyze the case studies of football clubs in five countries (Algeria, China, England, France, and Japan) in order to explore business models that are customized to and under influence of local conditions. Yeh and Taylor (2008) discuss governance in sports organizations focusing on the structure and roles of boards. Jacopin et al. (2013) analyze various business models of sports businesses in order to find their differences in relation to other types of businesses. Their analysis is conducted from the perspective of creating value. Bayle (2021) tells the story of the French Tennis Federation and attempts to analyze its dependence on the public sector.

### *Business models of electronic sports*

Scholz (2019) presents the emergence and development of eSports, discusses its principles, analyzes the stakeholders and makes predictions about the future of eSports. Vera and Terron (2019) analyze the business industry of electronic sports (eSports) giving focus to stakeholders and new business models. Felczak (2020) explores the case of Onet-RAS in order to "asses the process of strengthening the commercial potential of formalized eSports enterprises in a relatively new, national market" (Felczak, 2020, p. 177). Dwyer et al. (2019) study the differences between daily and season long fantasy sports and their consumption behaviors.

### Conclusions

In response to the first study question, it should be noted that research on business models in sports organizations and sport-related industries has been accumulating since 2004. However the significant increase in its productivity is very recent (2020–2021). The leading contributors to research production in the field are scholars from the United Kingdom, Spain, the United States, Germany, China, and Croatia. In response to the second study question, among the core references in the field are the studies on business models in fitness centers (García-Fernández et al., 2018) and F1 races (Aversa et al., 2015). In the most recent publications, works on adjusting sports organizations to the COVID-19 restrictions by Ratten (2020), and the coopetition strategies among small clubs by Crick and Crick (2020) are particularly nooteworthy. In response to the third study question, within the conceptual structure of the research field the four thematic clusters may be identified as the focus on: (1) various aspects of sport management, (2) business models in sport-related services, (2) business models and financial performance in sport, and (4) business model innovation in sport. In response to the fourth question, the following research fronts have been discovered: (1) business models of football clubs, (2) financial performance of football clubs' business models, (3) business models in sports other than football, (4) relationships with investors and sponsors, (5) business models of amateur/ non-profit clubs, (6) business models of sports organizations in the COVID-19 context, (7) business models of sports facilities, (8) business models in sports tourism, (9) business models in sports media and betting companies, (10) sports organizations' branding and their relationships with fans, (11) governance and value creation in sports organizations, (12) business models of electronic sports.

In discussing the findings of this study, the limitations of the research process should be taken into account. First, dependence on one source of bibliometric data, i.e. Scopus, should be noted. Although Scopus is widely recognized as a high quality database, it is biased toward publications written in English, which may mean that some valuable works published in languages other than English are omitted. Second, restricting the search to publications that contain a conjunction of the terms 'business model' and 'sport' may be considered quite narrow in the wider context of sports businesses and organizations. As there is no commonly accepted agreement about what sports businesses really are and as the sports system includes commercial but also non-profit and public organizations, the use of the word 'business' may sometimes not be appropriate and some authors would use other keywords (e.g. 'governance model' or 'performance model'). Consequently, some valuable publications may have been lost in the sampling process. However, because these alternative keywords may not fit all the requirements of a business model and in order to remain strictly in line with the focal theme of the edited collection, narrow searching criteria were employed. Third, due to the very dynamic development of the field in recent years, which is expected to continue, there is a risk of the findings becoming outdated. It seems reasonable and necessary to propose replicating the study after about five years. Fourth, because the identification of research fronts was based on the combination of bibliographic coupling and systematic literature review, some degree of subjectivity may have influenced the process of categorizing the selected publications into research fronts.

Taking into account the findings of the study, three avenues for further research may be identified. First, as the studies of business models of football clubs are over-represented in comparison to other sports, scholars are encouraged to shift their research to contexts other than football. Second, due to the disruptive changes in the business environment of sports organizations caused by the COVID-19 pandemic and related restrictions, studies on the shifts and adjustments in business models of these organizations should be continued. Third, the consequences of digitalization processes on business models of sports organizations and sport-related service industries need to be explored.

## Acknowledgments

The author is grateful to Dr Mateusz Tomanek from Nicolaus Copernicus University in Toruń, Poland and Prof. Dr Mathieu Winand from LUNEX International University of Health, Exercise and Sports, Differdange, Luxembourg for their comments and suggestions for improving the quality of the manuscript.

## References

Abere, A., Bronsteen, P., & Elzinga, K. G. (2012). The economics of NASCAR. In L. H. Kahane & S. Shmanske (eds), *The Oxford Handbook of Sports Economics: The Economics of Sports* (Vol. 1) (pp. 319–333). Oxford University Press. https://doi.org/10.1093/OXFORDHB/9780195387773.013.0017

Aghaei Chadegani, A., Salehi, H., Md Yunus, M. M., Farhadi, H., Fooladi, M., Farhadi, M., & Ale Ebrahim, N. (2013). A comparison between two main academic literature collections: Web of Science and Scopus databases. *Asian Social Science, 9*(5), 18–26. https://doi.org/10.5539/ass.v9n5p18

Amara, M., Henry, I., Liang, J., & Uchiumi, K. (2005). The governance of professional soccer: Five case studies – Algeria, China, England, France and Japan. *European Journal of Sport Science, 5*(4), 189–206. https://doi.org/10.1080/17461390500344503

Aversa, P., Furnari, S., & Haefliger, S. (2015). Business model configurations and performance: A qualitative comparative analysis in Formula One racing, 2005–2013. *Industrial and Corporate Change, 24*(3), 655–676. https://doi.org/10.1093/ICC/DTV012

Baena-Arroyo, M. J., García-Fernández, J., Gálvez-Ruiz, P., & Grimaldi-Puyana, M. (2020). Analyzing consumer loyalty through service experience and service convenience: Differences between instructor fitness classes and virtual fitness classes. *Sustainability, 12*(3), art. 828. https://doi.org/10.3390/SU12030828

Bayle, E. (2021). La gouvernance de la Fédération Française de Tennis entre 1970 et 2020: Entre autonomie et dépendances dans. *Movement and Sports Sciences – Science et Motricite, 111,* 21–36. https://doi.org/10.1051/sm/2021007

Bennike, S., Storm, R. K., Wikman, J. M., & Ottesen, L. S. (2020). The organization of club football in Denmark – A contemporary profile. *Soccer and Society, 21*(5), 551–571. https://doi.org/10.1080/14660970.2019.1690472

Bonaut-Iriarte, J. & Vicent, M. (2020). El origen de la televisión deportiva de pago en España: El caso de la lógica programática de Canal plus (1990–2005). *Estudios Sobre El Mensaje Periodistico, 26*(2), 429–440. https://go.gale.com/ps/i.do?p=IFME&sw=w&issn=11341629&v=2.1&it=r&id=GALE%7CA625707789&sid=googleScholar&linkaccess=fulltext

Booth, A., Sutton, A., & Papaioannou, D. (2012). *Systematic Approaches to a Successful Literature Review.* Sage.

Borges, F. (2019). Soccer clubs as media organizations: A case study of Benfica TV and PSG TV. *International Journal of Sport Communication, 12*(2), 275–294. https://doi.org/10.1123/IJSC.2019-0001

Börner, K., Chen, C., & Boyack, K. W. (2003). Visualizing knowledge domains. *Annual Review of Information Science and Technology, 37*, 179–255. https://doi.org/10.1002/aris.1440370106

Boyle, R. (2015). Battle for control? Copyright, football and European media rights. *Media, Culture and Society, 37*(3), 359–375. https://doi.org/10.1177/0163443714567020

Bradbury, T., Mitchell, R., & Thorn, K. (2021). Moving forward: Business model solutions for amateur sport clubs. *Managing Sport and Leisure, 26*(3), 189–205. https://doi.org/10.1080/23750472.2020.1734479

Buzzelli, N. R., Gentile, P., Billings, A. C., & Sadri, S. R. (2020). Poaching the news producers: The Athletic's effect on sports in hometown newspapers. *Journalism Studies, 21*(11), 1514–1530. https://doi.org/10.1080/1461670X.2020.1763191

Caldas, D., Cruz, E. F., & da Cruz, A. M. R. (2020). Time2Play – Multi-sided platform for sports facilities: A disruptive digital platform. *ICEIS 2020-Proceedings of the 22nd International Conference on Enterprise Information Systems, 2*, 269–277. https://doi.org/10.5220/0009412902690277

Callon, M., Courtial, J. P., & Laville, F. (1991). Co-word analysis as a tool for describing the network of interactions between basic and technological research: The case of polymer chemistry. *Scientometrics, 22*(1), 155–205. https://doi.org/10.1007/BF02019280

Callon, M., Courtial, J. P., Turner, W. A., & Bauin, S. (1983). From translations to problematic networks: An introduction to co-word analysis. *Social Science Information, 22*(2), 191–235. https://doi.org/10.1177/053901883022002003

Casadesus-Masanell, R. & Campbell, N. (2019). Platform competition: Betfair and the UK market for sports betting. *Journal of Economics and Management Strategy, 28*(1), 29–40. https://doi.org/10.1111/JEMS.12310

Casadesus-Masanell, R. & Ricart, J. E. (2010). From strategy to business models and onto tactics. *Long Range Planning, 43*(2–3), 195–215. https://doi.org/10.1016/j.lrp.2010.01.004

Casadesus-Masanell, R. & Ricart, J. E. (2011). How to design a winning business model. *Harvard Business Review, 89*(1–2), 100–107.

Cortsen, K. (2013). Annika Sörenstam – a hybrid personal sports brand. *Sport, Business and Management: An International Journal, 3*(1), 37–62. https://doi.org/10.1108/20426781311316898

Cortsen, K. (2017). 'Re-branding' women's football by means of a new sports product: A case study of women's football in Denmark. *Soccer and Society, 18*(7), 1058–1079. https://doi.org/10.1080/14660970.2015.1133410

Crick, J. M. & Crick, D. (2020). Coopetition and sales performance: Evidence from non-mainstream sporting clubs. *International Journal of Entrepreneurial Behavior and Research, 27*(1), 123–147. https://doi.org/10.1108/IJEBR-05-2020-0273

Czakon, W. (2011). Metodyka systematycznego przeglądu literatury. *Przegląd Organizacji, 3*, 57–61. https://doi.org/doi:10.33141/po.2011.03.13.

Di Minin, A., Frattini, F., Bianchi, M., Bortoluzzi, G., & Piccaluga, A. (2014). Udinese Calcio soccer club as a talents factory: Strategic agility, diverging objectives, and resource constraints. *European Management Journal, 32*(2), 319–336. https://doi.org/10.1016/J.EMJ.2013.04.001

Di Simone, L. & Zanardi, D. (2020). On the relationship between sport and financial performances: An empirical investigation. *Managerial Finance*, *47*(6), 812–824. https://doi.org/10.1108/MF-09-2020-0478

Dilys, M. & Gargasas, A. (2014). Structural business model based on cooperation between sports organizations and sponsors. *Engineering Economics*, *25*(1), 94–102. https://doi.org/10.5755/J01.EE.25.1.2680

Donohue, J. C. (1974). *Understanding Scientific Literature: A Bibliometric Approach*. MIT Press.

Dwyer, B., Drayer, J., & Shapiro, S. L. (2019). To play or not to play? An analysis of dispositions, gambling, and daily fantasy sport. *Journal of Sport Management*, *33*(3), 174–188. https://doi.org/10.1123/JSM.2018-0115

Escamilla-Fajardo, P., Alguacil, M., & García-Pascual, F. (2021). Business model adaptation in Spanish sports clubs according to the perceived context: Impact on the social cause performance. *Sustainability*, *13*(6), art. 3438. https://doi.org/10.3390/SU13063438

Escamilla-Fajardo, P., Parra-Camacho, D., & Núñez-Pomar, J. M. (2021). Entrepreneurship and resilience in Spanish sports clubs: A cluster analysis. *International Journal of Environmental Research and Public Health*, *18*(10), art. 5142. https://doi.org/10.3390/IJERPH18105142

Evens, T., Lefever, K., Valcke, P., Schuurman, D., & Marez, L. De. (2011). Access to premium content on mobile television platforms: The case of mobile sports. *Telematics and Informatics*, *28*(1), 32–39. https://doi.org/10.1016/J.TELE.2010.05.004

Felczak, M. (2020). Local eSports media analyzed through the circuit of culture framework: Onet-RAS case study. *CEUR Workshop Proceedings*, *2637*, 177–187.

Fortunato, J. A. (2013). Television broadcast rights: Still the golden goose. In P. M. Pedersen (ed.), *Routledge Handbook of Sport Communication* (pp. 202–210). Routledge. https://doi.org/10.4324/9780203123485-28

García-Fernández, J., Gálvez-Ruíz, P., Fernández-Gavira, J., Vélez-Colón, L., Pitts, B., & Bernal-García, A. (2018). The effects of service convenience and perceived quality on perceived value, satisfaction and loyalty in low-cost fitness centers. *Sport Management Review*, *21*(3), 250–262. https://doi.org/10.1016/J.SMR.2017.07.003

Guo, D., Chen, H., Long, R., Lu, H., & Long, Q. (2017). A co-word analysis of organizational constraints for maintaining sustainability. *Sustainability*, *9*(11), art. 1928. https://doi.org/10.3390/su9101928

He, Q. (1999). Knowledge discovery through co-word analysis. *Library Trends*, *48*(1), 133–159.

Herold, E., Boronczyk, F., & Breuer, C. (2021). Professional clubs as platforms in multi-sided markets in times of COVID-19: The role of spectators and atmosphere in live football. *Sustainability*, *13*(4), 1–16. https://doi.org/10.3390/su13042312

Holzmayer, F. & Schmidt, S. L. (2020). Financial performance and corporate diversification strategies in professional football – Evidence from the English Premier League. *Sport, Business and Management: An International Journal*, *10*(3), 291–315. https://doi.org/10.1108/SBM-03-2019-0019

Hutchins, B., Rowe, D., & Ruddock, A. (2009). "It's fantasy football made real": Networked media sport, the internet, and the hybrid reality of MyFootballClub. *Sociology of Sport Journal, 26*(1), 89–106. https://doi.org/10.1123/SSJ.26.1.89

Huth, C. (2020). Who invests in financial instruments of sport clubs? An empirical analysis of actual and potential individual investors of professional European football clubs. *European Sport Management Quarterly, 20*(4), 500–519. https://doi.org/10.1080/16184742.2019.1684539

Jacopin, T., Kase, K., & Urrutia, I. (2013). Value creation and performance criteria for sport entities. In S. Gómez, K. Kase, & I. Urrutia (eds), *Value Creation and Sport Management* (pp. 22–59). Cambridge University Press. https://doi.org/10.1017/CBO9780511762765.003

Jenkins, I. & Rios-Morales, R. (2013). Market niches and the perceptual economic impacts on a remote alpine village: The BRITS Week in Laax. *Event Management, 17*(3), 299–310. https://doi.org/10.3727/152599513X13708863378033

Johnson, M. W., Christensen, C. M., & Kagermann, H. (2008). Reinventing your business model. *Harvard Business Review, 86*(12), 50–59.

Kessler, M. M. (1963). Bibliographic coupling between scientific papers. *American Documentation, 14*(1), 10–25. https://doi.org/doi:10.1002/asi.5090140103

León-Quismondo, J., García-Unanue, J., & Burillo, P. (2020a). Análisis de importancia-valoración (Ipa) y modelo kano aplicados a centros fitness de la comunidad de Madrid. *Cultura, Ciencia y Deporte, 15*(44), 233–234. https://doi.org/10.12800/ccd.v15i44.1464

León-Quismondo, J., García-Unanue, J., & Burillo, P. (2020b). Best practices for fitness center business sustainability: A qualitative vision. *Sustainability, 12*(12), art. 5067. https://doi.org/10.3390/SU12125067

Litvishko, O., Veynberg, R., Ziyadin, S., Sousa, R. M. D., & Rakhimova, G. (2019). Professional sports: Strategic approaches to investment attractiveness formation. *Economic Annals-XXI, 178*(7), 105–113. https://doi.org/10.21003/EA.V178-09

López-González, H., Stavros, C., & Smith, A. C. T. (2017). Broadcasting sport: Analogue markets and digital rights. *International Communication Gazette, 79*(2), 175–189. https://doi.org/10.1177/1748048517694969

Maltese, L. & Veran, L. (2013). Managing and modelling the combination of resources and global brands in international sporting events. *International Journal of Business and Globalisation, 11*(1), 19–44. https://doi.org/10.1504/IJBG.2013.055314

Manfredi Sánchez, J.-L., Rojas Torrijos, J.-L., & Herranz de la Casa, J.-M. (2015a). Innovación en el periodismo emprendedor deportivo: Modelo de negocio y narrativas. *Profesional de La Informacion, 24*(3), 265–273. https://doi.org/10.3145/EPI.2015.MAY.06

Manfredi Sánchez, J.-L., Rojas Torrijos, J.-L., & Herranz de la Casa, J.-M. (2015b). Periodismo emprendedor: El periodismo deportivo en España. *Revista Latina de Comunicacion Social, 70*, 69–90. https://doi.org/10.4185/RLCS-2015-1035

Martín-Guart, R., Lopez-Gonzalez, H., & Fernández-Cavia, J. (2017). El deporte como antídoto contra la fragmentación de audiencias: Un estudio exploratorio de los programas más vistos de la televisión en España

(1989–2016). *Revista Latina de Comunicacion Social, 72*, 1027–1039. https://doi.org/10.4185/RLCS-2017-1206

Maxcy, J. G. (2013). Rapidly advancing technology and policy choices: Transforming the economic landscape of the sport media. In P. M. Pedersen (ed.), *Routledge Handbook of Sport Communication* (pp. 485–495). Routledge. https://doi.org/10.4324/9780203123485-59

Mazur, Z. & Orłowska, A. (2018). Jak zaplanować i przeprowadzić systematyczny przegląd literatury. *Polskie Forum Psychologiczne, 23*(2), 235–251. https://doi.org/10.14656/PFP20180202

McNamara, P., Peck, S. I., & Sasson, A. (2013). Competing business models, value creation and appropriation in English football. *Long Range Planning, 46*(6), 475–487. https://doi.org/10.1016/J.LRP.2011.10.002

Moher, D., Liberati, A., Tetzlaff, J., & Altman, D. G. (2009). Preferred reporting items for systematic reviews and meta-analyses: The PRISMA statement. *BMJ, 339*(7716), 332–336. https://doi.org/10.1136/BMJ.B2535

Perechuda, I. (2020a). Utility of financial information in managing football business model: Case from Central Eastern Europe. *Journal of Physical Education and Sport, 20*, 1257–1264. https://doi.org/10.7752/JPES.2020.S2175

Perechuda, I. (2020b). Intellectual capital determinants of football clubs in Europe. *Polish Journal of Sport and Tourism, 27*(2), 8–13. https://doi.org/10.2478/PJST-2020-0008

Perić, M., Durkin, J., & Vitezić, V. (2018). Active event sport tourism experience: The role of the natural environment, safety and security in event business models. *International Journal of Sustainable Development and Planning, 13*(5), 758–772. https://doi.org/10.2495/SDP-V13-N5-758-772

Perić, M. & Slavić, N. (2019). Event sport tourism business models: The case of trail running. *Sport, Business and Management: An International Journal, 9*(2), 164–184. https://doi.org/10.1108/SBM-05-2018-0039

Perić, M., Vitezić, V., & Đurkin Badurina, J. (2019). Business models for active outdoor sport event tourism experiences. *Tourism Management Perspectives, 32*, art. 100561. https://doi.org/10.1016/J.TMP.2019.100561

Perić, M., Vitezić, V., & Mekinc, J. (2016). Conceptualising innovative business models for sustainable sport tourism. *International Journal of Sustainable Development and Planning, 11*(3), 469–482. https://doi.org/10.2495/SDP-V11-N3-469-482

Perić, M., Vitezić, V., & Mekinc, J. (2019). Comparing business models for event sport tourism: Case studies in Italy and Slovenia. *Event Management, 23*(3), 379–397. https://doi.org/10.3727/152599518X15403853721466

Perić, M. & Wise, N. (2015). Understanding the delivery of experience: Conceptualising business models and sports tourism, assessing two case studies in Istria, Croatia. *Local Economy, 30*(8), 1000–1016. https://doi.org/10.1177/0269094215604131

Perić, M., Wise, N., & Dragičević, D. (2017). Suggesting a service research agenda in sports tourism: Working experience(s) into business models. *Sport, Business and Management: An International Journal, 7*(1), 58–76. https://doi.org/10.1108/SBM-09-2015-0031

Pittz, T., Bendickson, J. S., Cowden, B. J., & Davis, P. E. (2020). Sport business models: A stakeholder optimization approach. *Journal of Small Business and Enterprise Development*, *28*(1), 134–147. https://doi.org/10.1108/JSBED-12-2019-0409

Porter, A. L., Kongthon, A., & Lu, J.-C. C. (2002). Research profiling: Improving the literature review. *Scientometrics*, *53*(3), 351–370. https://doi.org/10.1023/A:1014873029258

Prado-Román, M., Prado-Román, A., Plaza-Casado, P., & Paz-Gil, I. (2019). Public's behaviour in front of sports: Case of Spanish football. *Studies in Systems, Decision and Control*, *180*, 214–224. https://doi.org/10.1007/978-3-030-00677-8_18

Price, D. J. de S. (1965). Networks of scientific papers. *Science*, *149*(3683), 510–515. https://doi.org/10.1126/SCIENCE.149.3683.510

Quansah, T., Frick, B., Lang, M., & Maguire, K. (2021). The importance of club revenues for player salaries and transfer expenses – How does the coronavirus outbreak (COVID-19) impact the English Premier League? *Sustainability*, *13*(9), art. 5154. https://doi.org/10.3390/SU13095154

Ramchandani, G., Shibli, S., & Kung, S. P. (2018). The performance of local authority sports facilities in England during a period of recession and austerity. *International Journal of Sport Policy*, *10*(1), 95–111. https://doi.org/10.1080/19406940.2017.1420676

Ratten, V. (2020). Coronavirus disease (COVID-19) and sport entrepreneurship. *International Journal of Entrepreneurial Behavior and Research*, *26*(6), 1379–1388. https://doi.org/10.1108/IJEBR-06-2020-0387

Reid, G. (2017). A fairytale narrative for community sport? Exploring the politics of sport social enterprise. *International Journal of Sport Policy*, *9*(4), 597–611. https://doi.org/10.1080/19406940.2017.1349827

Rodriguez-Pomeda, J., Casani, F., & Alonso-Almeida, M. del M. (2017). Emotions' management within the Real Madrid football club business model. *Soccer and Society*, *18*(4), 431–444. https://doi.org/10.1080/14660970.2014.980736

Santacruz Lozano, J. A., Mateos, M. E., Remón, A. C., & Jiménez-Beatty Navarro, J. E. (2021). Spanish sport facilities: Differences between public and private, and according to their business model. *Retos*, *39*, 38–45. https://doi.org/10.47197/retos.v0i39.74842

Scholl, H. J. & Carlson, T. S. (2012). Professional sports teams on the Web: A comparative study employing the information management perspective. *European Sport Management Quarterly*, *12*(2), 137–160. https://doi.org/10.1080/16184742.2012.670254

Scholz, T. (2019). *eSports is Business: Management in the World of Competitive Gaming*. Palgrave Pivot. https://doi.org/10.1007/978-3-030-11199-1

Schotten, M., El Aisati, M., Meester, W. J. N., Steiginga, S., & Ross, Cameron, A. (2017). A brief history of Scopus: The world's largest abstract and citation database of scientific literature. In F. J. Cantú-Ortiz (ed.), *Research Analytics: Boosting University Productivity and Competitiveness through Scientometrics* (pp. 31–58). Auerbach Publications. https://doi.org/https://doi.org/10.1201/9781315155890

Teece, D. J. (2010). Business models, business strategy and innovation. *Long Range Planning*, *43*(2–3), 172–194. https://doi.org/10.1016/j.lrp.2009.07.003

Tranfield, D., Denyer, D., & Smart, P. (2003). Towards a methodology for developing evidence-informed management knowledge by means of systematic review. *British Journal of Management, 14*(3), 207–222. https://doi.org/10.1111/1467-8551.00375

van Eck, N. J. & Waltman, L. (2010). Software survey: VOSviewer, a computer program for bibliometric mapping. *Scientometrics, 84*(2), 523–538. https://doi.org/10.1007/s11192-009-0146-3

van Eck, N. J. & Waltman, L. (2020). *VOSviewer Manual.* https://www.vosviewer.com/documentation/Manual_VOSviewer_1.6.15.pdf

Vera, J. A. C. & Terrón, J. M. A. (2019). The esports ecosystem: Stakeholders and trends in a new show business. *Catalan Journal of Communication and Cultural Studies, 11*(1), 3–22. https://doi.org/10.1386/cjcs.11.1.3_1

Waśkowski, Z. & Jasiulewicz, A. (2021). Consumer engagement using digital technologies in the process of co-creating consumer value in the sports market. *Journal of Physical Education and Sport, 21*(S2), 1131–1141. https://doi.org/10.7752/jpes.2021.s2143

Wemmer, F., Emrich, E., & Koenigstorfer, J. (2016). The impact of coopetition-based open innovation on performance in nonprofit sports clubs. *European Sport Management Quarterly, 16*(3), 341–363. https://doi.org/10.1080/16184742.2016.1164735

Wilson, R., Plumley, D., & Barrett, D. (2015). Staring into the abyss? The state of UK rugby's super league. *Managing Sport and Leisure, 20*(6), 293–310. https://doi.org/10.1080/23750472.2016.1141367

Wise, N., Perić, M., & Đurkin, J. (2019). Benchmarking service delivery for sports tourism and events: Lessons for Gorski Kotar, Croatia from Pokljuka, Slovenia. *European Journal of Tourism Research, 22*, 107–128.

Wiśniewski, A. (2021). Sport club business model. *Journal of Physical Education and Sport, 21*(S2), 999–1005. https://doi.org/10.7752/jpes.2021.s2124

Yeh, C. M. & Taylor, T. (2008). Issues of governance in sport organisations: A question of board size, structure and roles. *World Leisure Journal, 50*(1), 33–45. https://doi.org/10.1080/04419057.2008.9674525

Yi, S., Lee, Y. W., Connerton, T., & Park, C.-Y. (2021). Should I stay or should I go? Visit frequency as fitness centre retention strategy. *Managing Sport and Leisure, 26*(4), 268–286. https://doi.org/10.1080/23750472.2020.1763829

Yu, J.-G., Jeong, Y.-D., & Kim, S.-K. (2021). Verifying the effectiveness of sports event policies for a city's sustainable growth: Focusing on the multiple effects. *Sustainability, 13*(6), art. 3285. https://doi.org/10.3390/su13063285

Zhu, J. & Liu, W. (2020). A tale of two databases: The use of Web of Science and Scopus in academic papers. *Scientometrics, 123*(1), 321–335. https://doi.org/10.1007/s11192-020-03387-8

Zott, C., Amit, R., & Massa, L. (2011). The business model: Recent developments and future research. *Journal of Management, 37*(4), 1019–1042. https://doi.org/10.1177/0149206311406265

Zupic, I. & Čater, T. (2015). Bibliometric methods in management and organization. *Organizational Research Methods, 18*(3), 429–472. https://doi.org/10.1177/1094428114562629

# 3 Digital Models of Business Excellence Based on the Example of Sports Organizations

*Wojciech Cieśliński and Mateusz Tomanek*

## Introduction

Nothing develops an organization like change and one possible changes is the transformation of the organization into a digital business model. Sport is one of the objects and subjects of research in the context of digitization. Change is needed in this area because services need to be competitive, whether they are located in professional or amateur sports and sporting recreation. The idea of digitization is not a qualified organizational measure. It is a necessity resulting from the development of digital technologies and their use in improving the effectiveness of the functions of a sports organization.

Digitization is a process – the acquisition of data, conversion to a form of information and the generation of the knowledge necessary for decision-making, *i.e.*, its use at the appropriate time and place. The idea associated with digital transformation comes down to defining what the added value of this process is. It is assumed that it is knowledge and streaming its flows. Acquiring data and transforming them into information does not generate added value (Bazewicz, Collen, 1995; Cieśliński, 2011). Sportspersons, coaches, managers, fans, and sports sponsors need only the knowledge that will allow them to consciously participate in a training and sporting spectacle, and that helps sponsors to make decisions about sponsorship opportunities.

Digitization is a process in which an organization becomes an algorithm and managing it means processing data that the algorithm (machine processing) transforms into information (Bazewicz, Collen, 1995). A cognitive approach drawn from evolutionary theory (Stańczyk-Hugiert, Gorgól, 2012) implies the application of a research methodology confirming the evolutionary development of an organization towards digital maturity, namely through birth, growth, and improvement phases. This chapter presents contemporary research directions in

DOI: 10.4324/9781003270126-4

the field of digital models of business excellence based on the example of sports organizations.

Axiologically, the broadly understood concept of satisfaction in sport, *i.e.*, the creation of value for which the customer will be willing to pay, was adopted as a research consideration (Cieśliński, 2011). In particular, the efficiency and pressurization aspects (Łasiński, 1998) of research on satisfaction in sport are understood here as positively evaluated effects (*i.e.*, effectiveness). In the studies described, satisfaction is ultimately defined as an assessment of the quality of the activities of sports organizations (Tomanek, 2019), which contribute to the creation of value for sponsors, sportspersons, and fans. The subject of the study is organizational modelling and it is assumed that sports organizations aim to create value for key stakeholders as the most important aspect of satisfaction in sport.

The aim of the research is to identify, describe, and explain, as well as design, digital business models in sport, with specifications for digital models of excellence, exemplified by research into the digital maturity of organizations. The specific objective is to describe organizational modelling processes in light of the digital transformation of sports organizations. Of particular interest are the processes of embedding sports business in the organizational space of sports, digital models of sports business, and digital models of business excellence, using the author's own method of diagnosing the processes of digital transformation, *i.e.*, the digital maturity of sports organizations.

The research question underpinning this chapter is how digital models of business excellence can fit into the organizational development of sports institutions and clubs, allowing effective implementation of activities related to satisfaction in sport. To this end, studies on phases of organizational development measured by digital maturity were designed and conducted (Cieśliński, 2011, 2020). Digital models of business excellence provide an answer to the fundamental question, i.e., what actions should be taken in order to achieve high quality and satisfaction from participation in sport for stakeholders in sports organizations. To this end, research on the level of organizational development of sports clubs was designed from a perspective of cognitive evolution (Cieśliński, 2020) and levels were measured using a research tool to ascertain the digital maturity of organizations (Cieśliński, 2011, 2020). From this perspective, digital models of business excellence provide answers to the following questions:

1  Do clubs use data and message streaming (and to what extent)?
2  What is the saturation level of digital tools in sports clubs?

3 What is the conversion rate from real to digital resources?
4 What is the level of convergence of real, digital and media processes in sports clubs?
5 What is the level of implementation of gamification mechanisms in sports clubs?

Answers to these questions should enable researchers to find out whether the features of digital models of business excellence in sports clubs have a real impact on stakeholders' achievement of high quality activities and satisfaction with participation in sports.

The chapter describes the process of organizational modelling in the field of embedding sports organizations in a digital organizational space, assuming that, like any other organization, they function in real, virtual and media organizational spaces. The chapter assumes that, for these activities, it is both necessary and indispensable to acknowledge the trajectory of civilized development, which is towards the digital transformation of the organization (Cieśliński, 2020), *i.e.*, the use of modern ICT technologies and their conduciveness to the creation of new values and their flows in the organizational space of sport (Cieśliński, Głowicki, 2017).

The chapter describes activity models that create new business models in sport, fostering a continuous process of quality improvement and generating new values and streaming value chains and their flows to new areas related to satisfaction in sport. Models of aligning sports organizations with digital models of business excellence are outlined, with a view to improving the effectiveness of stakeholders' satisfaction with participation in broadly defined processes and events carried out by sports organizations.

The chapter presents digital models of sports business and the resulting digital models of business excellence, which are exemplified from empirical research in which the author's own method of researching the digital maturity of organizations (Cieśliński, 2020) is here applied to sports organizations. The structure of the work therefore entails a description of what a sports organization is (it is based on case studies, which will serve as reference models for the following chapters), the organizational space of sport, and digital business models, as well as a description of digital business excellence models in sport (Figure 3.1).

The organizational modelling of the processes of embedding and anchoring digital business models in the so-called 'organizational space of sport' is described and designed below, as are the cognitive aspects of digital business models in sport.

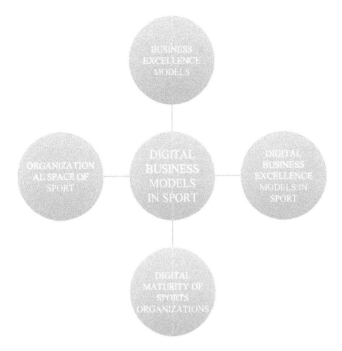

*Figure 3.1* Research structure.

## The organizational space of sport

As indicated in the introduction, the subject of this research is organizational modelling of the processes of digital transformation of sports business. The processes of digital transformation of business must be focused on activities that will allow the organization to locate itself in an optimal place (space of place) and time (space of time) for the sports business, allowing for free movement (space of flows) (Cieśliński, 2018a), depending on where and when the possibility of taking over the value arises. In a nutshell, the organizational space of sport is formed by the relationships that arise in a place and time that generate value for sportspersons, fans, and sponsors (Figure 3.2).

The essence of the establishment of business in an organizational space is the flow of values that arise in a specific place (a sportsperson during training and competition), at a specific time (a fan participating in the sporting event) and with a specific dynamic flow of these values, *i.e.*, how the potential sponsor perceives the sporting event and the sportspeople themselves at the point of considering whether to financially support the sporting business.

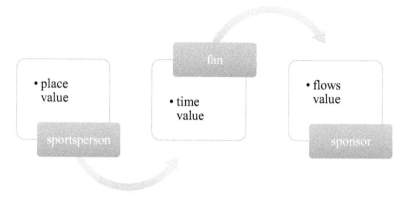

*Figure 3.2* Model of processes embedding business in the organizational space-time of sport.

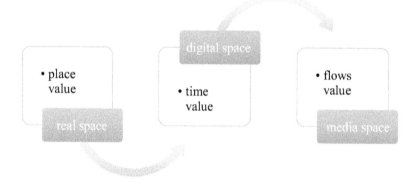

*Figure 3.3* Model of streaming value chains by embedding sports business in different dimensions of an organizational space.

The space of place, time, and flow can be streamed between three pillars; real, virtual (here digital) and media space. Figure 3.3 offers a model for embedding sports organizations, indicating that the real space is primarily where value is generated (in sports hall, entertainment hall, or wherever sports competitions are held). Virtual space is primarily the point at which the sportsperson, coach or sports manager generates value in the form of data, information and knowledge about methods of sports training and/or competition. A media space is a flow of values generated by social media, which in turn is a basis for sponsorship decisions (Figure 3.3).

At its simplest, organizational space can be defined as a set of relations and interactions between objects and people and technologies. Organizational space is created by organizational and inter-organizational networks of relations. Organizational space be both tangible and intangible (researchers define it as virtual and media – while other researchers also perceive it as a network of human relations (Sztompka, 2016). Time space indicates that events are subject to dynamics. They have their causes in the past, others are in the present and some may generate effects in the future. Space of place is an indication that events have an effect locally (within an organization), regionally, and globally. Time space, in turn, generates new effects that are not measurable in terms of results. Organizational space is influenced by real, virtual, and media events. Hence we are talking about real, virtual, and media organizational space.

Today, sport and its organization are not only real, but also virtual, and include the media. The development of sports organizations is the result of the development of ICT and media technologies. The real dimension is the physical activity of a sportsperson, and its value lies in health and the sporting level. In the virtual dimension, the most important element is data (about sportspeople, fans, and sponsors) and its value lies in the possibility of transforming data into information and knowledge (Cieśliński, 2020). In the media space of the sports organization, the most important element is the data from which the value of media recognition, sportspersons, fans, and sponsors can be estimated (Kloc, Tomanek, Cieśliński, 2019).

> Civilisation does not work as it wants, but as it must. Why should we develop cybernetics properly? Among other reasons, because soon we will probably come across an 'information barrier' that will hamper the growth of science if we don't make the mental overturn that has been made in the field of manual work over the last two centuries.
>
> (Lem, 2013)

## Business models in sport

The business model, which according to Porter (2001) is a description of the activities of the company that provide it with profit, is used by every organization, including sports ones. Other definitions of the business model include 'a story that explains how an enterprise works', 'an idea for a company to make money' (Koźmiński, 2004, p. 123), a 'description of how a traditional enterprise operates', or 'representing how business creates and delivers value for both customers and the enterprise'. Thanks to the many perspectives provided by researchers such as S.M. Shafer, H.J. Smith and J.C. Linder, and based on analysis of 12 definitions of business models, 42 key words were identified from these definitions, which have been arranged into four groups:

- strategic choices – customers, value proposition, skills, revenues, competitors, offer, strategy, branding, diversification and mission,
- value creation – resources and assets, processes and activities,
- value generation – costs, profits, financial aspects,
- value network – suppliers, customer information, customer relations, information, product and service flows (Koźmiński, 2004, p. 123).

However, looking at the sports industry, where B2B and B2C relations take place and where the clubs' income comes from both business (sponsorship) and fans (tickets), it is worth focusing mainly on the following business models:

- Crowdfunding – the outsourcing of project financing to a group of supporters. In this model, an organization or other entity relies on the will and willingness of customers, fans, or viewers to voluntarily support a specific idea. An example can be the action taken by Skra Bełchatów for the renovation of the volleyball players' locker room, or the Lech Poznań fan club, where money was collected for murals that will immortalize the characters who have made the club's history.
- Freemium – an extremely popular model in the Internet age. It assumes free access to a given service with the possibility to purchase additional functionalities. In Poland, this is not the domain of sports clubs, but rather (rarely) TV signal providers, where the provider shares profits with sports organizations.
- Open Business – the collaboration of different entities in order to work out the most innovative solutions. This model assumes great openness and transparency of the organization which decides to make its activities available and encourage other companies, which are also its competitors, to cooperate. Business clubs established in sports organizations are the first step to such activities, which later result in, among other things, marketing alliances strengthening the position of cooperating brands.
- Subscription model – a one-time user fee for goods or services, paid regularly. This model gives reassurance not only to the customer (who does not have to make repeated transactions), but also to the organization, which has the ability to plan for its revenues

with precision. It is often the case that an organization applies the techniques contained in a given model, not fully knowing its theoretical basis. For this model, one can point to the use of sponsorship agreements (B2B) or passes (B2C).

## Digital business models in sport

The fourth industrial revolution (Industry 4.0) is a term applied to rapid transition to digital working, in which the organization should be treated as an algorithm and management as a process of data processing. Digital organization can therefore be summarised as modern technologies implementing their basic functionalities, including algorithmization of the organization and data processing as a new way of management. There is a hypothesis that it is the satisfaction derived from participation in sport that determines involvement, and thus active participation, in it. Digitization generates innovation, streames value chains and allows their flow in real time (streaming mechanism). Technologies cannot replace humans; their function is to support cognitive processes in research into digital business models in sport. The basic function of new technologies is to support the processes of sports training and the organization of the work of sports clubs, including that sports events. These functions can be reduced to one common denominator, namely the streaming of value chains based on the latest information and communication technologies and social media. This means that technologies can contribute to the generation of new values, such as automation of data acquisition, machine processing it into useful information, and information flow and diffusion of knowledge through social networks and mobile ICT systems. The functions of modern technologies should be primarily to improve the efficiency of meeting the needs and expectations of sportspeople, supporters and sponsors, increasing the level of satisfaction these entities have from participating in sport. Contemporary sport requires new models of operation. Depending on who is the beneficiary of sports services, business models of sports organizations are changing. Mass sports, amateur and professional sports, elderly sports, children's and young people's sports, and disabled sports are different models of action and adopted business models in sports organizations. The structure of the study is presented in a matrix below, which describes the main research areas (Table 3.1).

These models have been described from the perspective of the three main stakeholders in the sports business, namely: sportspeople, fans, and sponsors. In this studies, the research consideration is primarily

*Table 3.1* Sport satisfaction matrix – problems and research structure

| Entities/models | Business models | Digital business models and business excellence models |
|---|---|---|
| Sportspeople | Quality of the sports training process | Orientation towards data acquisition, processing and provision |
| Fans | Attractiveness of a sporting event | Orientation towards knowledge provision |
| Sponsors | Media value of the club, of the sportsperson, and of the sporting event | Orientation towards message delivery |

the satisfaction these stakeholders gain from participating in sport and analysis of business models primarily covers the social aspects of return on investment. The subject of this analysis will be IT, ICT and social media in general, and particularly smart watch technologies, mobile applications such as Endomondo, Runastic and smart phones as a device to monitor our daily activities, and the impact of social media on the creation of sports activities.

The business model in sport offers a way for organizations to compete in the marketplace for sports services. Models of business excellence in sport respond to the quest for answers on how to improve levels of service quality and satisfaction with participation in sport and, in turn, digital models of business excellence in sport (Cieśliński, 2020) seek answers to the question of how ICT can help in the development and improvement of activities to create a high level of quality and satisfaction in sport.

Indicators measuring the degree of satisfaction in sport may include the digital maturity of sports organizations in terms of the degree and effectiveness of ICT use in sport's organizational. The essence of this research therefore boils down to answering the fundamental question of whether and to what extent Digital Business Excellence Models in sport can improve the quality of activities in this area, in particular access to sports services and events, and can result in improved participant satisfaction with sports activities or events.

Business excellence in this chapter comes down to redefining classical models into digital models. Measured with the help of the organization's digital maturity, the levels of organizational development from the perspective of using modern digital tools have made it possible to describe modern/traditional business models using digital tools in the most efficient way. As Stanisław Lem (2013) says in his book, entitled 'Summa Technologikae' (first published in 1964), it is not technology but new theories of cognition and the resulting recommendations for practice that can determine the development and effective application of dynamically developing information technology.

Digital models of excellence are available in all kinds of sport, both professional and amateur, and also sport for the disabled and the elderly.

## Digital business excellence models in sport

The digital sports business model is primarily about managing data, information and knowledge. Modern technologies used in the management of sports organizations concern their acquisition, processing, and delivery (Figure 3.4).

Digital business models extend traditional value chains through the use of modern IT and ICT technologies. When describing a digital sports business model it should be noted that a large element of the services is provided in an automated way, with the Internet used to communicate and create media value, and the possibility of personalizing the service offer of a sports organization for individual participants (sportspeople, fans, sponsors). The service, or its rendering, can be provided using mobile applications (Cieśliński, Głowicki 2017). A new perspective on the organization of sports clubs and companies is generated by the development of these new IT and ICT technologies

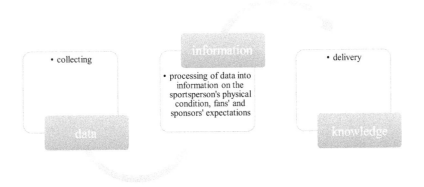

*Figure 3.4* Target model of digital sports organization.

(Koźmiński, 2004, pp. 123–124). Business models using them are among the elements generating new ways of competing in the sports services market. They are supplemented by social media, which have become a new tool for communication strategies and promotion of the sports events and products sold by sports organizations. Figure 3.5 presents a business model using advanced information and communication technologies.

Modern information and communication technologies (IT, ICT, social media), allow for effective management of an organization's activities in the area of data, information, and knowledge. Figure 3.6

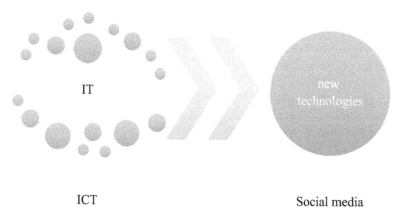

IT

new technologies

ICT                                   Social media

*Figure 3.5* Sports Business Model (SBM) – a new technology.

data

flow of values

information                           knowledge

*Figure 3.6* SBM – the flow of values perspective.

presents a sports business model based on the flow of values understood here as transforming data into information and knowledge.

The precise identification of the key factors of sports success from the perspective of the target groups' satisfaction with participation in this business, is an important element of Sports Business Models (SBMs). One of the most popular schemes used to analyse and create business models is the Business Model Canvas, developed by the Swiss, Alexander Osterwalder, in 2008. The use of this model allows (Osterwalder et al. 2010):

- development of a credible and accurate business promotion strategy,
- precise identification of key business areas,
- the possibility of locating weak points even before moving on to business,
- preparation of a clear presentation of the idea,
- development of a credible and accurate business promotion strategy.

There are different classifications of business models. For example, Michael Rappa (2004, 2010) has distinguished the following: Brokerage Model, Advertising Model, Infomediary Model, Merchant Model, Manufacturer Model, Affiliate Model, Community Model, Subscription Model and Utility Model.

Models of business excellence therefore come down to a common denominator – internal and external customer satisfaction. It can be said that the paradigm 'satisfaction of the sportsperson, fan and sponsor adopted in the research on Digital Business Excellence Model in sport can be the direction of a continuous process of improving the activities of sports organizations in search of ways to satisfy the above mentioned entities in active participation in sport. The key success factors (KSF) in building the target SBM include a model based on the satisfaction of players, fans, and sponsors that is:

- the sportsperson model,
- the fan model,
- the sports sponsor model (Figure 3.7).

Business excellence in this model assumes that everything is focused on the satisfaction of the three target groups. Business excellence is nothing more than the possibility of continuous improvement and comparison with others according to the world standards adopted here. A sports results orientation (professional sport), sports activity

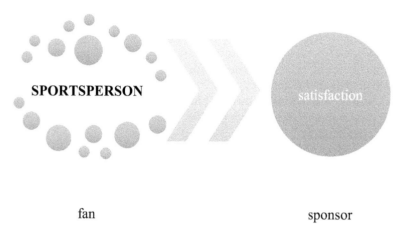

fan                              sponsor

*Figure 3.7*  Business excellence model in sport – target groups.

orientation (amateur sport), fan involvement through the attractiveness of a sporting spectacle and sports sponsor orientation, achieving high media value for a sportsperson, sports club, or event may be competitive advantages for a sports organization. Satisfaction with participation in sport therefore boils down to the results expected by individual entities. A professional sportsperson expects high sporting results, and a professional amateur sportsperson expects a full spectrum of services in their sporting activity. A fan, in turn, expects a high level of attractiveness in a sporting event in which he or she participates, and a sponsor expects high media value, so that his/her financial and/or barter share is covered by the media value obtained by the sports club (Kloc, Tomanek, Cieśliński, 20; Figure 3.8).

Digital models of excellence cover many aspects, from customer service (sportsperson, fan, sponsor), through the organization of a sports event to monitoring social, media, and business effects. Digital models, as previously described, primarily use modern digital tools and social media to stream flows of value (flows of real-time data, information, and knowledge), with these tools being used to implement gamification mechanisms (real-time assessment of the effectiveness of sports behaviour during sports training, competition and the media value of the show). These tools also make it possible to use machine processing to analyse a large amount of data on a sportsperson's behaviour during sports training and competition, as well as the level of satisfaction of the fan and sponsor with participation in a sports event (Figure 3.9, see also Figure 3.11).

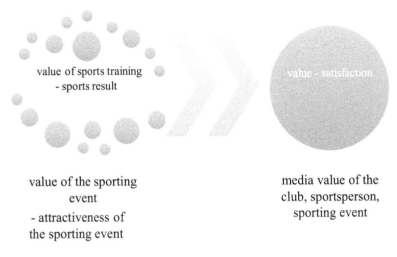

value of sports training
- sports result

value - satisfaction

value of the sporting
event
- attractiveness of
the sporting event

media value of the
club, sportsperson,
sporting event

*Figure 3.8* SBM – the value perspective.

SPORTSPERSON           FAN            SPONSOR

*Figure 3.9* Digital business excellence models in sport.

The theory of business excellence models is based on quality systems. However, in this chapter 'quality' is not the exclusive preserve of scientific prediction. The models of excellence described here have their source in the classical approach to building models, but are primarily related to the description and explanation of the development of these models, as accelerated by the digital development of the economy, organizations, society, and civilization in line with the industry 4.0 model. The research therefore includes a description of traditional business excellence models based on quality systems and the functionalities of modern information technologies inscribed in those models that are making the 'revolutionary' shift towards digital business excellence models. Digital business excellence models are primarily the

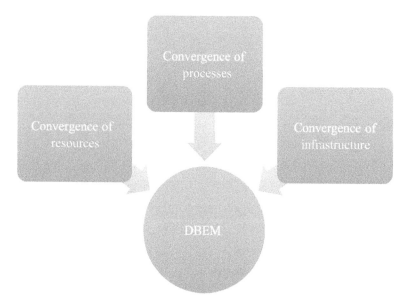

*Figure 3.10* SBM – Digital Business Excellence Model – Level 1.

results of studies (Cieśliński, 2018, 2018a) concerning the digital maturity of an organization, namely:

1  the need to convert resources from analogue to digital
2  the necessity for convergence of the organization's business processes
3  the need for convergence of the organization's information technology infrastructure (Figure 3.10).

These activities make it possible to achieve the following organizational mechanisms as digital excellence, namely:

1  streaming flows of values
2  gamification
3  machine processing (Figure 3.11).

The following list is an overview of the definitions of the main concepts used in the study, their description and explanation: organizational space, business models, models of excellence, and digital models including the digital maturity of the organization. These concepts constitute a cognitive-methodological reference point for describing and explaining the issues analysed in terms of a satisfaction problem

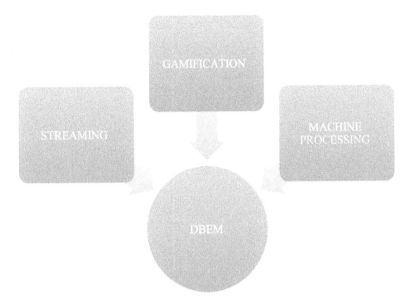

*Figure 3.11* SBM – Digital Business Excellence Model – Level 2.

in sport. They contribute to the search for an answer to the question of what business model a sports organization should adopt in order to be competitive in the market for sports services in terms of satisfaction from practising a sport, watching a sports spectacle and sponsor satisfaction. The Business Excellence Model (BEM) and the Digital Business Excellence Model (DBEM) are derived from the business model adopted (BM; Figure 3.12).

'Values' refers to the sportsperson, fan, and sponsor. Quality is determined by BEMs and DBEMs. It is the business model that determines the direction of a sports organization towards a continuous improvement process and DBEMs, or organizational improvement in the search for the modern ICT technologies that will aid achievement of satisfaction.

A business model in sport that is based solely on the satisfaction of the most important stakeholders is not sufficient to enable a sporting organization to achieve success, because the sportsperson, fan, and sponsor expect something else. The model needs to be made more specific by defining the directions in which the organization needs to improve in order to fully satisfy these stakeholders. Digital business excellence models depend on the answer to the question: What technologies can be used to improve the satisfaction of the sportsperson,

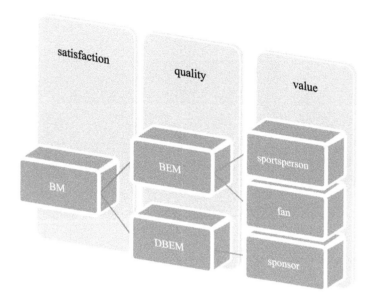

*Figure 3.12* SBM – Business model as an indicator of sports organisation activities.

fan, and sponsor in a sporting event? In order to answer this question, it is necessary to define the business models adopted by a sports organization and the directions of improvement of the business, *i.e.*, the business excellence models of sports organizations.

Industry 4.0, business models, business excellence models, quality in sport and the methodology of researching organizational development towards digital transformation, *i.e.*, the digital maturity of an organization, set the post-modern, dynamic directions for the development of contemporary sport, understood as a phenomenon with a high degree of ambiguity, impossible to describe with two-value logic. Industry 4.0 was created on the basis of evolution, *i.e.*, from the application of mechanization (steam engine), through electrification to the creation of digital models of operation and the Internet and the total integration of people, things and objects. Services 4.0 can be defined as the product of evolution from simple physical contacts between the seller and the buyer, through digitization to services through tools such as the Internet of All Things and Virtual and Augmented Reality or AI and machine processing without any human involvement as a seller (human involvement being reduced to writing an algorithm). Google, FB, and platforms integrating sellers and buyers lead to improved flexibility,

*Table 3.2* The stakeholder deployment matrix in different organizational spaces of sport

| Stakeholders/ types of OSS | Real | Virtual (digital) | Media |
|---|---|---|---|
| Sportspeople | Training | Digital support | Image creation |
| Fans | Participating in a sports event | Analysis of the event | Media value – active participation |
| Sponsors | Sponsorship contract | Provision of knowledge | Media value – passive participation |

efficiency, and greater competitiveness of services. These are the features of Service 4.0.

Sport, including the organizational space of sport, is a network of relations (Chomiak-Orsa, 2013, Cieślinski, Głowicki, 2017) which is made up of sports stakeholders (sportspeople, fans, sponsors). Organizational networks are created in real, virtual, and media space (Table 3.2).

Sports, physical activity, sports spectacles, fans and sponsor participation form networks of relations. The coupling of relations created in real, virtual (digital) and media space at the psychophysical (sportsperson training), social (fans) and business (sponsors) levels is impossible to describe using two-value description logic. While this research covers digitization, it also includes quality and satisfaction in sport, as exemplified in the research conducted by Tomanek (2019). The organizational space of the research described in this chapter, is that of excellence models in sport (Cieśliński, Głowicki, 2017) and it covers:

1  the carriers of business excellence in sport.
2  entities of influence (broadly defined as sport stakeholders).
3  the roles played by stakeholders in particular types of value carriers (Table 3.3).

Sport primarily has a social dimension. Active participation in sports and sporting events, and sponsoring sporting events are dimensions of the so-called 'mass culture' (*profanum*). Unlike *sacrum* (high culture), it motivates a significant proportion of societies' populations due to the fact that men and women are 'social animals' whose physical activity is inscribed in their evolution. This activity is a manifestation of the 'spiritual' involvement of the body in motion, as an actual manifestation of spiritual activity. Through sport, people enter into social relations and meet their basic needs for physical activity.

*Table 3.3* Space for digital models of excellence in sport

| Carriers of excellence/entities of influence | Sportspeople | Fans | Sponsors |
| --- | --- | --- | --- |
| Social | Active entry into the relationship | Passive entry into the relationship | Relationship capital |
| Media | Media value | Media value carrier | Expected media value |
| Business | Value of sports results and contracts | Cost incurred to participate in a sports event | Expected business value |

The digital business excellence model in sport entails full use of the development of digital technologies (electronic, information, and media devices) to develop and improve the evolutionary development of an organization's maturity so that it can assimilate modern technologies in the provision of sports services for its own needs.

Digital Business Excellence Models (DBEMs) address the following opportunities in particular:

1  the implementation of gamification mechanisms.
2  the implementation of potential streaming flows of values between stakeholders of the organizational space of sport.
3  conversion of analogue resources into digital form.
4  potential for implementing the mechanism of processing and machine learning.
5  potential for implementing mechanisms allowing the convergence of business processes carried out in the organizational space of sport, including the processes of sports training, organization of sports events, and social, media and economic value management processes.
6  potential for implementing mechanisms of convergence of organizational infrastructure of sport.
7  potential for using the latest technological trends conducive to achievement of the business objectives of sports organizations.

'Summa Technologiae' by Stanisław Lem in 1964 (2013) is an attempt to look at new directions of development from the perspective of cybernetics, which is the science of information theory and a methodological-epistemological interpretation of the development of modern information and communication technologies. The digital transformation of organizations takes place in human minds and not in the technological sphere. It is not new technologies that will revolutionize the organization but, above all, new ways of thinking. This thinking runs in a continuum between algorithm and heuristics, between data and knowledge, between talking about action and decision-making and action and decision-making.

> ...such a replacement will probably happen, but it will open up new paths, today only vaguely perceived. Not in the narrow sense that workers and technicians will be replaced by programmers of digital machines, because next generations, new species of these machines will no longer require programmers.
>
> (Lem, 2013, p. 66)

The new robot species will not need programmers because they will reprogram themselves when they are intelligently looped.

> ...one of the young Soviet astrophysicists, Kardashev, divided, during the aforementioned conference, hypothetical civilisations into three types, including, among the first, earth-like civilisations (annual energy consumption of about 4*1019 erg), the second, civilisations consuming energy of about 4*1033 erg, and the third, 'super-civilisations', which have mastered their galaxies with energy (energy of about 4*1044 erg). At the same time, the time necessary for the emergence of a civilisation and type was estimated at several billion years (following the example of the earth), the transition from type i to type ii would take only a few thousand years (an estimate based on the rate of increase in the energy production of the earth in recent centuries), and from type ii to type iii - would take several tens of millions of years. This last finding has met with criticism from other experts, as - at such 'rates of psychogenesis' - practically all galaxies would have to have their 'super-civilisations' already.
>
> (Lem, 2013, pp. 70 and 124)

It is not the development of technology, but the development of basic research that will have an impact on the development of civilization, the digital business excellence model, and the way in which an enormous amount of information is managed. The current 'algorithms' loop reality, provide solutions, or solve a problem structured in a way that prevents a real solution to the problem. The binary reality is not a natural reality, it is described using two-value logic. Unfortunately, as long as reality is indefinite', its nature will be unknown, but at the same time this blurriness generates a greater potential for action than zero-one.

So how does 'digital reality' fit in with organizational reality? Well, it structures an already structured problem, it acquires, analyses and processes megabits of data into information, nothing more. We need to 'blur' zero-one reality and bifurcate the model of embedding an organization in the digital organizational space. Embedding as a process should end with anchoring and that is the basis on which a digital business model should be built with its parameters determined by broadly defined sport, including professional and amateur sport, sport for children and young people, the disabled and the elderly. This research does not define a particular type of sport, but uses selected examples. Description and explanation of these models and an attempt to model them is based on the following three aspects:

1  real organizational space for sport versus digital space
2  real sports business models versus digital models
3  real models of business excellence in sport versus digital models of excellence
4  media models, *i.e.*, the use of media technologies to create new models of business excellence in sport, complement the above.

The digital excellence of a sports organization entails providing knowledge to all stakeholders in a sports organization. Sports organization stakeholders should know about ways of training, preparation for the game, the place and time of the sporting event, and the media value of the sporting event.

To summarize the cognitive-methodological aspects of organizational modelling of digital business excellence in sport, its functions come down to:

1  **Planning** – the data streaming mechanism: determining what data, from what space and how to acquire it.
2  **Organization** – the ways and tools of transforming data into information. The essence of this function is to answer the question: What conversion mechanism should be used – machine, cognitive, creative? When it comes to data conversion, one can talk about machine processing and transformation into information, *i.e.*, one can talk about cognitive transformation, and when it comes to knowledge, one can talk about creative transformation. The most

important element of managing a digital organization is the way knowledge is diffused.

3 **Control** – these are ways of protecting data, information and knowledge from cyber-hackers.

4 **Motivation** – the most important element in the management of an organization is how to assess the effectiveness of work performance. The mechanism that can be used here is gamification, *i.e.*, real-time feedback, about what has been done well and what has been done badly and what the result of the work is.

Based on the cognitive and methodological aspects described and explained like this, a tool was developed to study the digital maturity of sports organizations.

## Conclusions

1 Cognitive and methodological aspects of research are a reference point in terms of interpreting the results of empirical research. Empiricism cannot be interpreted without reference to cognitive aspects.

2 Satisfaction in sport is an element of research on quality understood as satisfying defined and hidden needs.

3 Satisfaction lies in the quality and added value generated by the activities of sports organizations.

4 The stakeholders of sports organizations are sportspeople, fans, and sponsors.

5 Digital sports business models are methods of processing data, information and knowledge.

6 In the digital business excellence models of sports organizations knowledge is an added value.

7 The maturity of digital business models in sport is a tool for researching the organizational development of sport in relation to digitization.

8 The digital transformation of sports organizations comes down to implementation, the stream mechanism of data acquisition, machine processing, and the gamification mechanism of knowledge diffusion.

9 Digitization is a process allowing the streaming of value chains in sports organizations, including the optimization of sports training processes, the organization of events for fans and the acquisition of new sports sponsors.

## Acknowledgements

The research described above is drawn from four research projects carried out by Wojciech Cieśliński:

- Process Maturity of Companies 2008–2009 (continued until 2014), Ministry of Science and Higher Education, Project Manager,
- Pe-AZS, designing a mobile process management platform in Sports Clubs 2014–2016, MNiSzW, Project Manager,
- Augmented Reality in Improving Sports Technology in Judo, 2015–2017, Ministry of Science and Higher Education, Main Contractor,
- AZON – digitization of scientific resources of AWF Wrocław, 2017–2019, PO PC, NCBiR, Substantive Coordinator, Manager of Task 5.

In addition, Mateusz Tomanek wishes to acknowledge the grant received from the Faculty of Economic Sciences and Management of the Nicolaus Copernicus University in Toruń, for research on 'Sports organization management'.

## Bibliography

Bazewicz, M., Collen, A. (1995). *Podstawy metodologiczne systemów ludzkiej aktywności i informatyki.* Wrocław: Oficyna Wydawnicza Politechniki Wrocławskiej.
Chomiak-Orsa, I. (2013). *Zarządzanie kapitałem relacyjnym w procesie wirtualizacji organizacji. Podejście modelowe.* Wrocław: UE Wrocław.
Cieśliński, W. (2011). *Doskonalenie procesowej orientacji przedsiębiorstw. Model platformy treningu procesowego.* Wrocław: UE Wrocław.
Cieśliński, W. (2018). *Strumieniowanie przepływów wartości w przestrzeni organizacyjnej – w kierunku transformacji cyfrowe.* [In] M. Budzanowska-Drzewiecka, K. Czernek (eds). *Kierunki ewolucji nauk o zarządzaniu.* Kraków: Wydawnictwo Uniwersytetu Jagiellońskiego.
Cieśliński, W. (2018a). Cyfryzacja przestrzeni organizacyjnej – w kierunku streamingu. *Zeszyty Naukowe Uniwersytetu Szczecińskiego, Ekonomiczne Problemy Usług*, no 2 (131/1), pp. 79–90.
Cieśliński, W. (2020). Cyfrowa dojrzałość organizacji-założenia poznawcze i metodologiczne (Digital maturity of the organization – cognitive and methodological assumptions). [In] *Szkoła Letnia Zarządzania, Zeszyty Naukowe Uniwersytetu Łódzkiego* (on-line).
Cieśliński, W., Głowicki, P. (2017). *IT space organization – process orientation.* [In] P. Cabała, M. Tyrańska (eds). *Zarządzanie organizacjami w*

*społeczeństwie informacyjnym: organizacje, projekty, procesy.* Warszawa: Instytut Organizacji i Zarządzania w Przemyśle "ORGMASZ", pp. 121–128.

Kloc, M, Tomanek, M., Cieśliński, W. (2020). Social media and the value of contracts based on the example of the NBA. *Journal of Physical Education and Sport*, vol. 20, suppl. no 5, art. 416, pp. 3063–3069. DOI:10.7752/jpes.2020.s5416

Koźmiński, A.K. (2004). *Zarządzanie w warunkach niepewności. Podręcznik dla zaawansowanych.* Warszawa: PWN.

Łasiński, G. (1998). Strategia prezentacji w procesie efektywnego komunikowania się. [In] W. Strykowski (ed.). *Media a Edukacja. II Międzynarodowa Konferencja Naukowa.* Poznań: Wyd. eMPi2.

Lem, S. (2013). *Summa technologiae.* Copyright by Barbara i Tomasz Lem.

Osterwalder, A., Pigneur, Y., Clark, T. (2010). *Business model generation.* Hoboken, NJ: Wiley.

Porter, M.E. (2001). *Strategy and the Internet, Harvard Business Review on advanced strategy.* Boston, MA: Harvard Business School Corporation.

Rappa, M.A. (2004). The utility business model and the future of computing service, *IBM Systems Journal*, nr 43, 32–42.

Rappa, M.A. (2010). Business models on the web, http://digitalenterprise.org/models/models.html (08.08.2021)

Stańczyk-Hugiert, E., Gorgól, J. (2012). Elements of inter-organisational networks-aspects of organisation and management. [In] J. Niemczyk, E. Stańczyk-Hugiert, B. Jasiński (eds). *Inter-organisational networks. Contemporary challenges for management theory and practice* (pp. 109–118). Warsaw: C.H. Beck.

Sztompka, P. (2016). *Kapitał społeczny: teoria przestrzeni międzyludzkiej.* Kraków: Wyd. Znak.

Tomanek, M. (2019). *Zarządzanie jakością w sporcie (Quality management in sport).* Toruń: Nicolaus Copernicus University.

# 4 Business Model Shift toward Flexibility

*Adam Wiśniewski*

## Introduction

Modern enterprises are focused on the implementation of highly defined tasks. The pursuit of hyper-specialization leads to an observable kind of "tunnel vision" which, on the one hand, allows the individual to strive for excellence in the tasks entrusted to them. On the other hand, it often causes a failure to adapt in response to impulses from a turbulent environment.

Business models permit us, first of all, to identify what an enterprise is and what it is not. At the same time, they facilitate management and decision-making by those in power. In the literature produced so far, there is a noticeable trend toward emphasizing the advantages of striving for organizational flexibility. Consequently, it makes sense to explore the possibility of using flexible business models.

This chapter reviews the main ideas about business model flexibility. An attempt is made to classify the main determinants of its occurrence and consider the possibilities for enterprises to move from their current business models toward flexible versions.

## Business models

In the literature, the concept of a business model has been described many times, but authors have failed to agree on the meaning of this concept. Therefore, there is no single, generally accepted definition of a business model (Zott et. ll., 2010). The concept is considered fundamental for any organization (Magretta, 2002). At the same time, using a business model is equated with designing a structure that captures the key aspects of a sustainable new venture (Morris et al., 2006). S. Lambert (2008) points out that 'the business model concept was born out of the need to understand and explain these new ways of doing business.'

DOI: 10.4324/9781003270126-5

In studies dealing with the subject of business models, one of the dominant aspects is the ability to 'read' how enterprises earn money and provide more value to their clients than their competitors (Rappa 2000). A business model is not a description of a complex social system with all its actors, relations and processes. Rather, it describes the logic of a 'business system' for creating value that lies behind the actual processes (Petrovic et al., 2001). But creating value is not the key issue for the company. In order to survive it needs to capture the value from its offering to the customer. In market competition 'each party in a transaction attempts to capture for themselves the largest part of the value produced, and the resulting measure is company profit' (Oliński, Szamrowski 2016, p. 41).

A business model is a very close representation of reality (Salas-Fumás, 2009). The business model describes the creation and delivery of value between the different areas of the company through relationships (Osterwalder et al., 2005, p. 12). There is also research to suggest the significance of the business model as a driver of value. Kamoun (2008) points out that a business model becomes the blueprint for the way a business creates and captures value from new services, products, or innovations. For the purposes of this study, it is therefore assumed that a business model is a description of the operation, construction and dependence of a profit-generating production project (Wiśniewski, 2017).

**Sport's market characteristics**

Contemporary sport's market is a multimillion-pound/dollar business. It draws on clubs, customers (fans), suppliers, media and many other firms to create products and services that are desirable worldwide. Sznajder (2007) highlighted the universal characteristics of sport's market:

- Sports organizations are strongly diversified,
- They have more diverse goals than the goals of enterprises operating in other industries,
- Professional sports clubs compete with each other on the one hand and on the other are dependent on each other,
- Managers' decisions are subject to immediate comment from media and customers (fans),
- The sports market is a double-dual market – organizations operate simultaneously in the sports market (where individual consumers are the buyers of products) and in the advertising and sponsorship market (for institutional buyers), because the sales to individual clients cannot cover club expenses. That's why they

have to use both B2C (business-to-consumers) and B2B (business-to-business) models.

As for the further development there are five main trends (Deloitte, 2020):

1  The rise of women's sports;
2  The continued evolution of e-sports;
3  Legalized sports betting;
4  College athletes maximizing their short-term value;
5  5G and sports in the cloud.

Each of those trends requires the creation of new activities for existing sports organizations and that demands flexibility. Most can be implemented using digital resources, tools or platforms.

## Flexible business models

The volatility of the environment, the market size and its dynamics result in the need for organizations to adapt to the changes taking place. Contemporary markets are defined as hyper-competitive (D'Aveni, 1998). The growing number of enterprises in industries and the increase in competitiveness necessitate the ability to adapt and reorganize over a short period of time. Organizational flexibility comes in handy here as its meaning is closely linked to the concept of time: flexibility is not a static condition, but it is a dynamic process. 'Time is a very essential factor of organizational flexibility' (Volberda, 1998). At the same time, flexibility requires consideration of two key activities: exploration and application. Researchers (cf. Teece et al., 1997; Volberda et al., 2010) have emphasized that *exploration* usually requires removing existing methods of operation from the organization, while *application* is based on an organization's ability to ensure an appropriate level of consistency. Together, these are the pillars for creating flexibility. As Golden and Powell (2000, 373) point out, organizational flexibility should be considered in four dimensions:

- Time – the time the organization needs to react or develop a response to the changes taking place;
- Scope – the degree of adaptation of individual elements of the organization to changes in the environment;
- Purposefulness – the selection of an appropriate way to react to the changes taking place. An offensive response is not always

right. On the other hand, a defensive response can be effective in some circumstances;

• Impact area – considering the direction of the reaction. Will the activities be directed at the internal areas of the organization or the external environment?

Teece et al. (1997) stated that flexibility is based on some sort of balance between the exploration and application of assets. Volberda (1998) put forward a similar view, saying that organizational flexibility has its foundation in the capacity of management to exercise control and the organization's susceptibility to being controlled. In this scenario, flexibility has two dimensions: the managerial task and the design of the organizational task (1998: 97). As presented in Figure 4.1, flexibility needs to be adapted to environmental characteristics. Only then can it be sufficiently and adequately designed. In practice there may be different organizational forms at play in fostering flexibility. These forms may be rigid, planned, flexible, or chaotic. In Volberda's theory these forms are aligned with the lifecycle of the enterprise.

This approach is based on a two-dimensional concept of managerial tasks: controlling the organization and organizational design. It sets

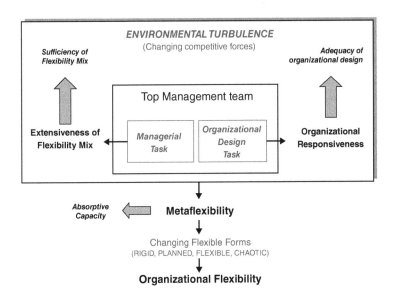

*Figure 4.1* Organizational flexibility.
Source: Based on Volberda (1998).

the challenges of developing dynamic capabilities that enhance flexibility and having adequate technology, structure and culture to utilize those capabilities (Volberda, Rutges, 1999). Efficient deployment of managerial tasks gives the company a sufficient flexibility, and when the organizational design task is well developed it has an 'adequate organizational design' (Volberda, 1998). The Figure also refers to the 'metaflexiblity' state. That is a managerial flexibility that represents the firm's support monitoring and learning systems. Metaflexiblity undertakes processing of information to support and facilitate the ongoing adjustment of management's flexibility and organizational conditions in line with environmental changes. The level of metaflexiblity determines access to new knowledge from the surrounding environment. The alignment of flexibility with the lifecycle was also the subject of research by Bhandari et al. (2004) on e-business. They created a list of requirements for flexibility and choices of strategic approach (Table 4.1).

This approach depends on a perspective in which requirements for flexibility and approaches to strategic choices depend on the lifecycle of a business. Three areas are taken into consideration for Startup/ Beta, customer acquisition, monetization and maturity phase: typical growth pattern, products/information gap and competitive position. When these are fully described and understood the so-called 'strategic imperatives' can be implemented. The first phase of a startup/beta is said to need a platform for rapid growth, with a strong team and a flexible site. These actions require a high quality product, technology and collaboration, governed by simple rules.

In the second phase, customer acquisition aims to build market share as quickly as possible by aggressively spending on partnerships and promotion. This needs a medium-level product and technology but a high degree of collaborativeness. The monetization phase allows for increasing revenues and customer lock-in by developing new revenue streams for the company. This requires a lower level of technology but medium levels of product and collaboration. It is dependent on dynamic capabilities. The maturity phase should be maintained to control firm's costs and optimize marketing expenditures in order to achieve profitable growth. Flexibility requirements here are low, and the strategy is focused on the industry's structure and resource base. As business advances, in time it acquires greater stability and raised expectations for consistent ROI, compared to earlier stages of the lifecycle where there are high levels of uncertainty and a high need for flexibility. Stavness and Schneider (2004), while considering workflow models, pointed out that there is a two-part classification that defines *flexibility by selection* and *flexibility by adoption*. They described flexibility by selection as

*Table 4.1* Requirements for flexibility and choice of strategic approach

| Lifecycle Stage | Startup/Beta 6 months–1 year | Customer Acquisition 1–2 Years | Monetization 2–5 years | Maturity > 5 years |
|---|---|---|---|---|
| Typical growth pattern | Exploiting niche opportunities in new markets/products | Extending product offerings and expanding markets | Increasing market share through complementary products and new markets | Defending market share growth by acquisition introduction of complementary products |
| Products/ information gap | High Market/ technical uncertainty, few products | Good knowledge of existing business, less known about new areas | Existing product lines, good knowledge of markets and technology | High knowledge of markets, wide range of products |
| Competitive position | Low industry power, susceptible to changes in the environment, relying on limited product offering | Low power in industry, vulnerable to drastic changes in environment | Medium degree of power, susceptible to juggernauts, specialists and sudden shifts in the environment | Substantial presence in industry, price maker, vulnerable to specialists |
| Flexibility requirements | High product High technology High collaborative | Medium product Medium technology High collaborative | Medium product Lower technology Medium collaborative | Lower product Lower technology Lower collaborative |
| Strategic approach | Simple rules | Simple rules/dynamic capabilities | dynamic capabilities | Industry structure/ resource based |

Increasing stability and expectations for consistent ROI

Increasing uncertainty and need for flexibility

Source: Based on Bhandari et al. (2004).

providing the user with some latitude in processing, with the availability of multiple pathways. Adoption, on the other hand, offers the ability to create new pathways through additional functionality and tools to change and integrate workflow types during runtime. Companies that exceed capacity often focus on the creation of flexible product and service offerings, dictated by new market specifics. The demands of the market are constantly changing, and specifics shift at both the micro and macro scale. Because of variability in supply, recipient needs - both the indirect and the so-called end-client ones - also change. Flexibility is thus the only way for business to 'stay alive'.

It is also said (Sanchez, Mahoney, 1996) that flexibility is the ability to reposition a firm in a market and to dismantle its previous strategies to meet new customer needs. Mason and Mouzas (2012) underline the linkage of flexibility and ambidexterity understood as capacity to simultaneously achieve alignment with current customer needs and adaptability to provide new customer solutions. De Toni and Tonchio (2005: 532) stated that there are four distinctive levels of strategic flexibility:

- strategic flexibility as the scope of the strategic options within a business;
- strategic flexibility as the speed of variation of the competitive priorities within a business;
- strategic flexibility as the variety of the possible new business;
- strategic flexibility as the swiftness of movement from one business to another.

To understand business model flexibility, it is first necessary to define the relevant level of its components (Mason, Mouzas 2012):

- The network level. The objective is to identify all available resources and capabilities for the company. The key is to know where and when to access and use them within their business network. Only then will their options to gain value be widened.
- The company level. Thanks to relationships between companies it is possible to obtain resources dictated by the customer's needs.
- The individual employee level. The baseline is the day-to-day solution of problems in the company. Managers need to have authority and responsibility to direct employees for effective work.

When the basis of flexibility is understood, it becomes clear that classical supply chains could be dispensed with. At every step, an organization should be prepared to identify, understand and adapt under the influence of stimuli from its environment. Creating products or services in a flexible way through a chosen business model is contingent on the market environment (Wei et al., 2017). Being able to adapt to changes is consistent with strategic concepts of flexibility that include the ability to sense major changes in surroundings that might have an impact on a company's business model (Johnson, 2003; Evans 1991). Second, it facilitates the ability to handle new resource requirements (Sanchez 1995; Pauwels, Matthyssens, 2004).

Business models are often defined as the concept of the modular structure of a firm. The best known example is the Business Model Canvas (Osterwalder, Pigneur, 2010). This type of definition permits analysis of certain areas of organization and fasten the flexibility changes. This strategic flexibility is also required for swift adjustments to business models. Within each model there are challenges to be faced (Schon, 2012). The first is to *manage competitive advantage.* The openness of some elements in business models could expose the business to copying by competitors. That is why the competitive advantage is so fragile and impermanent. The solution should be to build uniqueness and add supplementary value drivers to each element. The second challenge is to *sense the timing.* This is related to the lifecycle of an organization and the product or service on offer. A particular business model might be good today but worthless tomorrow. With a flexible approach, reaction time is shortened and new opportunities emerge. But bad timing could cause major damage. Reacting too fast can mean losing a current position of competitive advantage. Taking too much time creates an opportunity for other companies to build stronger positions. The last challenge faced is that of *ensuring structural innovation.* The risk is in coordinating different elements in the business model as these may become difficult to align. However, implementing flexibility within the elements of the model creates space to use outsourcing and transfers innovation potential to suppliers. It drives the organization to new boundaries and challenges it to become more innovative.

The organization's flexibility is often connected with digitalization. Here, the background for "doing a business" lies in being interconnected with the facilities provided by the Internet. Internet commerce gives rise to new types of business models. "That much is certain. But the web is also likely to reinvent tried-and-true models" (Rappa, 2000, p. 1). The Internet offers the possibility to widen the market for current operations or create new business. It refocuses the organization onto new customers or the new needs of existing customers.

The literature identifies two paths to respond effectively to customer needs (Mason, Mouzas, 2012). The first is to gain 'market focus'. This covers how companies identify and manage the demands of their markets. The second is to become 'network focused'. This approach tends to create or join interconnected companies who share information, knowledge, resources and tools for the common interest. Mason and Mouzas (2012) define four reasons to become network focused:

- The network can help to understand how market orientation can be transformed into a business model. Here it is important to remember that a new business model has an impact on other companies in the network.
- It makes visible the flexibility and limitations of an identified business model.
- Understanding market orientation improves understanding of business networks and aids better visualization and development of a flexible business model.
- Clarifying the interrelations in the network provides a new perspective for examining the previous theoretical background.

In effect, a manufacturing company starting with a classical approach to resource base production and ownership of tools (Table 4.1) needs to obtain a flexible business model that is compatible with network influence in order to become flexible (Figure 4.2).

The new flexible approach allows the creation of a business model that draws on the network (Figure 4.3).

*Figure 4.2* Resource-based manufacturing approach.

*Figure 4.3* Flexible network-based manufacturing approach.

The accessibility of the network is crucial. Gaining knowledge, re-sources, information, tools and experience from the network opens 'new doors' for the company. With this powerful backup the manufac-turer can become flexible and react to market needs. Only then does the 'firm's capability to identify changes in the environment, to quickly commit resources to new courses of action in response to changes and to act promptly when it is time to halt or reverse such resource com-mitments' grow (Yang et al., 2020, p. 772). When it has acquired its new flexibility, the organization faces a new challenge – maintaining this state. The organization that applied this system has to "maintain a competitive advantage and by so doing rely heavily on the outsourc-ing of capabilities and resources" (Sharma et al., 2010, p. 55). The clue is to "balance ... the need to maintain a connection to past concep-tions of the organization" (Gioia 1998, p. 21).

## Business model flexibility determinants

Starting from the analysis of studies focused on organizational flex-ibility, business models and environmental volatility, it is observable that researchers view their understanding of flexibility in the context of dependency on reasoning. They are in part focused on internal pro-cesses but some attach more importance to web flexibility. The first approach is interconnected with dynamic capabilities. The more dy-namic capabilities a company has, the more flexible it can be. Dynamic capabilities are based on three dimensions (Ansoff, Brandenburger, 1971): operational, structural and strategic. Flexibility in organiza-tion can be undertaken on operative, structural and strategic levels (Verdu-Jover, Gomez-Gras, Llorens-Montes 2008). Internal flexibility through dynamic capabilities allows a company to:

- create new offerings (products and services) and new processes (Teece, Pisano 1994),
- diversify the resource base and its integration, re-design, growth and independence,
- configure anew the resources needed for competitive advantage,
- adapt core competence over time (Upton 1994; Sanchez, 1995).

In the area of *organizational flexibility* there may be two main deter-minants: the degree of centralization and the formalization of the decision-making process (Hatum, Pettigrew 2006). Higher levels of centralization and formalization effect lower flexibility. Concentrated decision-making weakens a business and makes it difficult for the

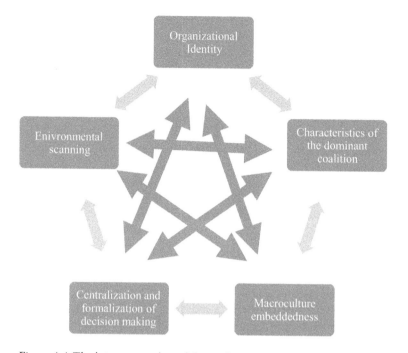

*Figure 4.4* The interconnection of determinants of organizational flexibility.
Source: Based on Hatum, Pettigrew (2007).

organization's members to participate in the decision-making process. The literature also identifies the determinants that can indirectly affect business model flexibility: low microculture embeddedness, heterogeneity of the dominant coalition, environmental scanning and strong organizational identity. More peripheral organizations are less engaged in dominant practices and more open to developing new ones (Greenwood, Hinings 1996). The stronger the organizational identity the less ready it is for change. In the area of *web flexibility*, a trend can be seen toward opening business models to other network participants. Hatum and Pettigrew emphasized network and flexible organizations' dependence on five determinants: organizational identity, characteristics of the dominant coalition, microculture embeddedness, centralization and formalization of decision-making and environmental scanning (Figure 4.4).

## Sport's clubs' flexibility

Within a theoretical context it is possible to ask 'How flexible can a sports' club be?' To answer this question a complex base of digital business model forms would be useful, separate from the contextual analysis of the above-mentioned determinants. This was offered in an article "klasyfikacje modeli biznesu" by Wiśniewski (2018). For the core business of a sports club, that is to provide training practice or prepare a team for participation in sports, there are few possibilities to adopt a flexible approach using digital resources. One way is for training to be implemented using the usual *subscription model* or *direct-to-customer model*. In both, a training course unit could be available via the Internet. In order to train, an athlete should subscribe or gain access to a digital platform with a set of training courses, so that they could train anywhere in the world. The *direct-to-customer model* offers individual solutions for each athlete, including live streaming supervision and consultation services.

A second core activity focused around participation in competitions could, at least partially, be digitalized using a flexible approach. These aspects could equally focus on activities accompanying performance. They could, for example, be used in a *virtual community model* that attracts fans wishing to access exclusive materials. Another approach would offer a *full-service* to provide a greater volume of information (e.g. live-stream statistics) or complementary activities (e.g. an OCR run could be complemented by discount offers or information on how to start training on your own).

## Conclusion

In a high-speed world, change is a turning point for the functioning of many enterprises. By introducing innovations, new offerings or expanding their businesses, organizations can ensure their survival and their ability to compete in the marketplace. Business flexibility facilitates reaction to changes and keeping up with the market at a relatively low cost. Key competences are the "star" that allows the development of a business model tailored to the market in which a company operates. However, it is important to remember that today's business model may not be appropriate tomorrow.

As this study shows, there are five key determinants of organizational flexibility: organizational identity, characteristics of the dominant coalition, microculture embeddedness, centralization and formalization of decision-making and environmental scanning. There are practically no markets where digital technologies are not used. All managers need to remember the constant need to look at features such as: time, scope, purposefulness and impact area, and this is applies to the sports market too. This study demonstrates the high importance of a flexible network-based approach. Even in traditional sports clubs, such an

approach can create new sources of income. In addition, it offers opportunities to enter new markets (for example, sports consulting or e-sport)
which, in the long term, may become the main source of income.

## Bibliography

Ansoff, H.I., Brandenburger, R.G. (1971), *A language for organization design:
Part I*, Management Science, vol. 17 (12), pp. 705–716.

Bhandari G., Bliemel M., Harold A., Hassanein K. (2004), *Flexibility in
e-business strategies: A requirement for success,* Global Journal of Flexible
Systems Management, vol. 5 (2), pp. 11–22.

D'Aveni, R.A. (1998), *Waking up to the new era of hypercompetition*, Washington
Quarterly, vol. 21 (1), pp. 183–195. http://dx.doi.org/10.1080/01636609809550302

De Toni A., Tonchia S. (2005), *Definitions and linkages between operational
and strategic flexibilities*, Omega. The International Journal of Management
and Science, vol. 33 (9), pp. 525–540. http://dx.doi.org/10.1016/j.omega.2004.
07.014

Deloitte. (2020), *2020 Sports industry outlook,* Deloitte Center for Technology, Media & Telecommunications

Evans J. (2007), *Strategic flexibility for high technology maneuvers – a conceptual framework,* Journal of Management Studies, vol. 28 (1), pp. 69–89.

Gioia D.A. (1998), *From individual to organizational identity* [in:] Whet-
ten D.A., Godfrey P.C. (eds), *Identity in Organizations: Building Theory
Through Conversations,* Thousand Oaks, CA: Sage, 17–32. http://dx.doi.
org/10.4135/9781452231495.n2

Golden W., Powell P. (2000), *Towards a definition of flexibility: In search of
Holy Grail?* Omega. The International Journal of Management, vol. 28 (4),
pp. 373–384. http://dx.doi.org/10.1016/S0305-0483(99)00057-2

Greenwood R., Hinings C.R. (1996), *Understanding radical organizational
change: Bringing together the old and the new intuitionalism*, Academy of
Management Review, vol. 21, pp. 1022–1054.

Hatum A., Pettigrew A.M. (2006), *Determinants of organizational flexibility: a
study in an emerging economy,* British Journal of Management, vol. 17, pp.
115–137. doi:10.1111/j.1467–8551.2005.00469.x

Hatum A., Pettigrew A. (2007), Can Argentinian companies survive? : a study
of the determinants of organizational flexibility [in:] Grosse R., Mequita
L.F. (eds), *Can latin American firms compete?*, Oxfotrd Press.

Johnson J.L. (2003), *Market-focused strategic flexibility: Conceptual advances
and an integrative model,* Journal of the Academy of Marketing, vol. 31 (1),
pp. 74–89. http://dx.doi.org/10.1177/0092070302238603

Kamoun F. (2008), *Rethinking the business model with RFID.* Communications
of the AIS, vol. 22 (1), pp. 635–658. http://dx.doi.org/10.17705/1CAIS.02235

Lambert S., (2008), *A conceptual framework for business model research,*
BLED 2008 Proceedings, vol. 24.

Magretta J. (2002), *Why business models matter?* Harvard Business Review, vol. 80 (5), pp. 86–92.

Mason K., Mouzas S. (2012), *Flexible business models,* European Journal of Marketing, vol. 46 (10), p. 1341. http://dx.doi.org/10.1108/03090561211248062

Morris M., Schindehutte M., Richardson J., Allen J. (2006), *Is the business model a useful strategic concept?* Journal of Small Business Strategy, vol. 17 (1), p. 28.

Oliński M., Szamrowski P. (2016), *The impact of EU funds on the development of a business model for small and medium-sized enterprises,* Olsztyn Economic Journal, vol. 11 (2), p. 169. http://dx.doi.org/10.31648/oej.2918

Osterwalder A., Pigneur Y. (2010), *Business Model Generation,* Edison, NJ: John Wiley & Sons Inc.

Osterwalder A., Pigneur Y., Tucci C.L. (2005), *Clarifying business models: Origins, present and future of the concept,* Communications of the Association for Information Systems, vol. 16, article 1.

Pauwels P., Matthyssens P. (2004), *Strategic flexibility in export expansion: Growing through withdrawal,* International Marketing Review, vol. 2 (4/5), pp. 496–510. http://dx.doi.org/10.1108/02651330410547162

Petrovic O., Kittl Ch., Teksten R.D. (2001), *Developing Business Models for eBusiness,* http://dx.doi.org/10.2139/ssrn.1658505 [Accessed: 10 August 2020]

Rappa M. (2000), *Business Models on the Web,* http://digitalenterprise.org/models/models.html [Accessed: 10 August 2020]

Sanchez R. (1995), *Strategic flexibility in product competition,* Strategic Management Journal, vol. 16, pp. 135–159.

Sanchez R., Mahoney T.J. (1996), *Modularity flexibility and knowledge management in product and organizational design,* Strategic Management Journal, vol. 17, pp. 63–76. http://dx.doi.org/10.1002/smj.4250160921

Salas-Fumás, V. (2009). *Modelos de negocio y nueva economía industrial,* Universia Business Review, (23), pp. 122–143.

Schon O. (2012), *Business model modularity – A way to gain strategic flexibility?* Controlling & Management, vol. 56, pp. 73–78. http://dx.doi.org/10.1365/s12176-012-0388-4

Sharma M.K, Sushil, Jain P.K. (2010), *Revisiting flexibility in organizations: Exploring its impact on performance,* Global Journal of Flexible Systems Management, vol. 11, pp. 51–68.

Stavness N., Schneider K.A. (2004), *Supporting Flexible Business Processes with a Progression Model,* MBUI.

Sznajder A. (2007), *Features of the professional sports market,* Gospodarka Narodowa, vol. 10, pp. 45–65.

Teece, D.J., Pisano, G. (1994), *The dynamic capabilities of firms: An introduction,* Industrial and Corporate Change, vol. 3 (3), pp. 537–556.

Teece, D.J., Pisano, G., Shuen, A. (1997), *Dynamic capabilities and strategic management,* Strategic Management Journal, vol. 18 (7), pp. 509–533.

Upton, D.M. (1994), *The management of manufacturing flexibility,* California Management Review, vol. 36 (2), pp. 88–104.

Verdu-Jover A.J., Gomez-Gras J-M., Lorens-montes F.J. (2008), *Exploring managerial flexibility: Determinants and performance implications*, Industrial Management & Data Systems, vol. 108 (1), pp. 70–86.

Volberda, H.W. (1998), *Building the Flexible Firm*, Oxford: Oxford University Press, http://dx.doi.org/10.1093/acprof:oso/9780198295952.001.0001

Volberda, H.W, and Rutges A. (1999), FARSYS: a knowledge-based system for managing strategic change, Decision Support Systems, vol. 26 (1), pp. 99–123.

Volberda, H.W., Foss, N.J., Lyles, M.A. (2010), *Perspective-absorbing the concept of absorptive capacity: How to realize its potential in the organization field*, Organization Science 21(4), pp. 931–951. http://dx.doi.org/10.1287/orsc.1090.0503

Wei Z., Song X., Wang D. (2017), *Manufacturing flexibility, business model design and firm performance*, International Journal of Production Economics, vol. 193, pp. 87–97. http://dx.doi.org/10.1016/j.ijpe.2017.07.004

Wiśniewski A. (2017), *Konstrukcja modeli biznesu*, AUNC. Zarządzanie, vol. 44 (2), pp. 75–85. http://dx.doi.org/10.12775/AUNC_ZARZ.2017.020

Wiśniewski A. (2018), *Klasyfikacje modeli biznesu, Research on enterprise in modern economy – Theory and practice*, Wydawnictwo Politechniki Gdańskiej, vol. 25 (2), pp. 33–50.

Yang D., Wei Z., Shi H., Zhao J. (2020), *Strategic flexibility and business model innovation*, Journal of Business & Industrial Marketing, vol. 35 (4), pp. 771–784.

Zott Ch., Amit R., Massa L. (2010), *The business model: Theoretical roots, recent developments and future research*, IESE Research Papers D/862, IESE Business School.

# 5 Challenges and Transformation of Football Clubs' Business Models

*Marlena Ciechan-Kujawa and Igor Perechuda*

## Introduction

Football has changed. Clubs continue to be part of the cultural and sentimental heritage of cities and regions, which continue to be passionate about them. But, beyond this cultural dimension, recent decades have been dominated by the importance of football's financial and media dimensions. The parallels between economics, finance and on pitch competitions are clear. As a business, the football economy has also been affected by global economic issues, especially in lower-tier clubs. We know that revenues come from ticket sales, sponsors and broadcasting rights, but it is not always easy to understand the business logic hidden behind them. The professionalisation of football and the emergence of investors as club owners have blurred clubs' objectives and profitability has emerged as an alternative aim. The appearance of two groups of objectives (sport and finance) has raised questions about their interrelations and the characteristics of football business models.

According to Sánchez et al. (2020), profitability and success on the pitch are connected in many ways. Sports success may lead to profits because wins attract fans to stadiums and increase media attention. It brings higher attendance and TV rights, and more interest from sponsors. All this leads to revenue increase but, despite that, many studies have pointed out that football costs over the same period have increased more rapidly (Barajas and Rodríguez, 2010; Szymanski 2017). Solberg and Haugen (2010) explained this phenomenon, using game theory, as the result of the necessity to secure scarce talent in order to win on the field. However, the rules of financial fair play could change the business models of football clubs.

Looked at from a different perspective, owners may make decisions that sacrifice sporting performance in order to increase profits, for

DOI: 10.4324/9781003270126-6

instance when a talented player is sold. This is the case in North American sports, with revenue-sharing and salary caps. Big teams sometimes refuse to compete to hire the top players, and stick with healthier financial performance (Einolf, 2004). Galariotis et al. (2018) also found that financial performance, measured in varying ratios, negatively affects sports performance in French football.

Another study (Sanchez et al., 2017) identified that clubs do not have their own objectives. Their aims depend on who their owner is. Some club owners do not worry about club finances but are concerned with the club's sports triumphs. But if, for example, we look at the Glazer family, we see that they did not buy Manchester United to enjoy attending club matches. Thus, we can see that a club's aims are determined by their owners and depend on that owners' preferences and structure. This is a complex subject because clubs with different objectives could participate in the same competitions and shareholders with different aims may invest in the same club.

The idea of the business model is a concept of business activity which describes the mechanisms of creating, delivering, and capturing value (Amit and Zott, 2001; Markides, 2006; Teece, 2010; Wirtz et al., 2016). It is a representation of the network of systems of a given organisation, of its resources and partners, its internal and external connections (Adner and Kapoor, 2010; Amit and Zott, 2015). While there are different approaches to defining and describing business models (cf. Casadesus-Masanell and Ricart, 2010; Demil et al., 2015; Massa et al., 2017; McGrath, 2010; Osterwalder and Pigneur, 2010), the key components are similar at a systemic level (Saebi et al., 2016). On the basis of the widely recognised approach of Osterwalder and Pigneur (2010), which is commonly referenced in professional literature, nine basic elements can be identified: customer segments, value propositions, distribution channels, customer relationships, revenue streams, key activities, key resources, key partners, and cost structure.

Chesbrough and Rosenbloom (2002), as well as Mitchell & Coles (2003), stress that business models are not stable over time and require not only constant adjustment to the changing environment but also the ability to anticipate the internal determinants of variability. It may be necessary to change the very concept of value creation (key resources, for instance), and also the structure of stakeholder interrelations or management mechanisms.

The structure of a business model is therefore the result of strategic choices concerning a combination of assets, policies, and the method of management (Casadesus-Masanell and Ricart, 2011). As many scholars have argued, the degree to which a business model is adjusted to current market requirements directly influences the level of competitiveness of a given organisation, the perceived value of its services, and the economic efficiency of the business (Amit and Zott, 2012; Anthony, 2012; Casadesus-Masanell and Ricart, 2010; Osterwalder et al., 2005). Flexibility in adjusting to these changes can, therefore, affect the success or failure of an organisation (Baden-Fuller and Haefliger, 2013; Brea-Solís et al., 2015).

In research literature, the triggers of business model change are sought primarily in external factors, and result from changes in either the macroeconomic or the competitive environment. Progress in the fields of information technology and communications is suggested to be the strongest factor involved in this phenomenon (Weill and Woerner, 2013; Wessel et al., 2016). However, other scholars emphasise the fact that companies often implement BM changes in response to the changing expectations of interested parties and their growing demand for CSR and sustainable development (e.g. Andries and Debackere, 2007; De Reuver et al., 2009; Doz and Kosonen, 2010; Ferreira et al., 2013; Johnson et al., 2008; Joyce and Paquin, 2016; Sabatier et al., 2012; Teece, 2010; Zollo et al., 2013). On the other hand, Foss and Saebi (2017) argue that modifications to the operational concept of an organisation are a necessary response to external interference, the globalisation of competitive processes, the pressure from existing competition, or the variability of the competitive environment, whereas Casadesus-Masanell and Ricart (2010), as well as Teece (2010), note the importance of changes pertaining to external regulation with regards to BM alteration.

In the case of soccer clubs, the main features that distinguish their business models from companies' business models, according to previous research, are mostly focused mostly on:

1   a utility approach. One of the most common objectives of football clubs is the maximisation of utility for stakeholders by maximising sport performance;
2   revenue maximisation instead of profit-orientation;
3   diverse ownership structures with different objectives (club members, private investors, public institutions, local government, etc.);
4   a strong influence on decision-making by stakeholders other than shareholders (e.g., public institutions which are often the co-owners of the club and owners of the infrastructure);
5   the high impact of intangible and vulnerable assets such as players;
6   the high share of HR costs in the costs structure;

7 the diverse and peculiar structure of revenues: television-broadcasting, sponsorship, ticket sales, player transfers, public funding (subsidies).

To sum up, the "competition" between sports results and financial stability is the key feature that distinguishes and disrupts the business of football, inspiring many studies in sport management.

Regulatory factors have been particularly relevant in the operation of European football clubs in the last decade. Implemented by UEFA in the 2013/2014 season, financial fair play (FFP) regulations have considerably changed the parameters of economic policy and the rules around a sustainable approach to the activities of clubs. The principles of FFP were intended as a solution to the significant financial difficulties of football clubs. Even before their implementation, the causes and mechanisms behind the paradox of very high-income organisations facing bankruptcy had been discussed by many scholars (e.g. Hamil and Walters, 2010; Solberg and Haugen, 2010; Szymanski, 2012). However, Szymanski (2012) has pointed out that this phenomenon is more typical of clubs in Europe than of those on other continents. Among the factors contributing to this situation, research has identified socio-cultural, managerial, legal, and economic issues.

The subject of socio-cultural conditions has been explored by Solberg and Haugen (2010) for instance. They have demonstrated that European football clubs compete more fiercely for talented players than professional teams on other continents, which supports the theory of Vrooman (1997) that, in order to achieve a better sports performance, European club owners are willing to forego a proper return on investment in financial terms.

On the other hand, Hamil and Walters (2010) focused on problems in the managerial area, in particular on the dissonance of the short-term financial planning of clubs in relation to their long-term investments. The researchers have also examined legal matters, pointing to a lack of proactive regulatory action aimed at solving the problem of chronic unprofitability and unsustainable debt, which may have resulted in a serious financial crisis in English football.

Among the identified financial mechanisms behind the difficulties faced by clubs, a key role was played by financial doping (excessive financing, not balanced by income, in order to cover losses arising from expenses on professional talent), resulting, in particular, in lack of payment for completed transfers or postponed salary payments (Hamil and Walters, 2010). It has also been pointed out that the financial problems of football clubs lie chiefly in the area of cost management

(Hamil and Walters, 2010); however, some scholars have emphasised the greater importance of a lack of correlation between revenues and expenses (Solberg and Haugen, 2010).

The objectives of FFP have been linked to licensing regulations and centred around the following issues described in art. 2.2 UEFA (2012):

a   to improve the economic and financial capability of the clubs, increasing their transparency and credibility,

b   to place the necessary importance on the protection of creditors and to ensure that clubs settle their liabilities with employees, social/tax authorities and other clubs punctually,

c   to introduce more discipline and rationality in club football finances,

d   to encourage clubs to operate on the basis of their own revenues,

e   to encourage responsible spending for the long-term benefit of football,

f   to protect the long-term viability and sustainability of European club football.

Therefore, the regulations concentrate on improving the financial management of clubs at a strategic level, and apply to those clubs which have reached the minimal threshold of revenues and expenses defined by UEFA after the 2011/2012 season. The intended effect of adhering to FFP is the achievement of a stable balance between revenues, expenses, and investments. The long-term prospects of financial management benefit from the method by which the financial situation of clubs is determined, among other factors. The break-even point became a key parameter in this evaluation, calculated by comparing the proper revenues from football activity with the costs of the main activity (player salaries and player acquisition depreciation). However, this is calculated on a rolling basis over a three-year period. This makes it possible to cover a potential deficit with profits from the previous year. The established rules – according to Scelles et al. (2019) – should also negate the effects of uncontrollable football results on financial outcomes. Simultaneously, the rules for financing club activity have been made stricter, as have the rules for monitoring payments to external and internal stakeholders, particularly employees, the state, or other football clubs (Articles 62, 65, 66). The regulations also specify what situations require the provision of additional financial information, such as those involving an auditor opinion or triggered by the status of important financial indicators (Articles 52, 62).

Since 2012, scholars have studied the topic of FFP every year. Up to the end of 2019, 48 indexed texts had been published in the Scopus database, mostly in the form of articles (44). The data used to analyse the publications in terms of FFP is presented in Table 5.1. In all categories, except for quotations, the threshold of three publications has been applied in selecting suitable texts. Quotations include research articles which have been referenced in at least 15 other publications indexed by Scopus.

*Table 5.1*  General publication profiling of the FFP research field

| Category | Top items (number of publications) |
| --- | --- |
| Country | United Kingdom (16); Germany (10); France (6); Greece (6); United States (5); Italy (3); Spain (3) |
| Source title | *International Sports Law Journal* (7); *Sport Business and Management an International Journal* (6); *International Journal of Sport Finance* (4) |
| Author | Schubert, M. (5); Dimitropoulos, P. (4), Flanagan, C.A. (3); Szymanski, S. (3) |
| Core references | Peeters and Szymanski (2014) (45); Müller et al., (2012) (38); Franck (2014) (31); Wilson et al. (2013) (27); Madden (2012) (24); Sass (2016) (20); Dimitropoulos and Tsagkanos (2012) (19); Drut and Raballand (2012) (19); Schubert and Könecke (2015) (17); Szymanski (2014) (17); Morrow (2013) (15); Ramchandani (2012) (15) |
| Subject area | Business, Management and Accounting (20); Social Sciences (17); Economics, Econometrics and Finance (15); Health Professions (5) |

Source: Own study based on data retrieved from Scopus (12 March 2020).

The impact of FFP has been analysed mostly by authors from the United Kingdom and Germany, while the works of four researchers – Schubert, Dimitropoulos, Flanagan, Szymanski – comprise over 30% of all sources. A third of the research has been published in three professional magazines: "*International Sports Law Journal*", "*Sport Business and Management an International Journal*" and "*International Journal of Sport Finance*". On the basis of keywords related to financial fair play, such as football, regulation, sport, UEFA, competition, competitive balance, corporate governance, and Europe, it is possible to identify the following author interests in specific topics:

1   The idea of FFP as well as the determinant factors and the organisational and legal effects of its implementation (e.g. Dimitropoulos, 2016; Menary, 2016; Morrow, 2013; Müller et al., 2012; Peeters and Szymanski, 2014; Sims, 2018).

2 The impact of the regulations on sports potential, club results, and competitiveness (e.g. Dimitropoulos and Scafarto, 2019; Franck, 2014; Peeters and Szymanski, 2014; Sass, 2016; Wilson et al., 2013).

3 The financial impact on internal and external stakeholders of implementing the regulations (e.g. Dimitropoulos and Scafarto, 2019; Franck, 2014; Peeters and Szymanski, 2014).

Across the discussion on FFP, a recurring theme is the adequacy of this concept for the purpose of assuring the long-term profitability and sustainable development of European football. There are significant research findings in this respect, in the form of studies that focus on presenting and measuring the effects of the changes introduced by FFP regulations in both the European football market and the business models of football clubs.

The rules of FFP were intended by UEFA to facilitate a more balanced competition in European football leagues. Vöpel (2011) and Sass (2012) have warned, however, that the UEFA regulations would "freeze" the hierarchy in European football, creating an entry barrier for investors. In addition, Peeters and Szymanski (2014) have raised the question of the potential effects of the break-even point restrictions stemming from FFP on a sharp decrease in average wages and salary-to-revenue ratio, resulting in the strengthening of the position of traditionally top-tier clubs. Sass (2016) has also demonstrated that the market size of a club has a positive influence on its historical success (greater success draws in more supporters, thus generating higher income, which facilitates further success and the growth of market size), which leads to a very unequal competition. The latest findings of Birkhäuser et al. (2019) lead to the conclusion that FFP rules have further increased competitive imbalance. According to the researchers, because of the barriers preventing new investors from entering and of the support for winners of the previous season in terms of budget shares in the following season, European football leagues are now less balanced and FFP has supported the current club hierarchy. This last opinion is shared by Gallagher and Quinn (2019) who assert that FFP regulations further increase the financial and athletic strength of elite clubs and potentially undermine the intensity of competition in the league, shifting the relative focus of clubs from sports productivity to financial productivity. Data analysis in a UEFA report (2019) indicates that during the period 2008–2017, the income share of the 12 largest clubs on the continent – Manchester United, Manchester City, Liverpool FC, Arsenal, Tottenham Hotspur, Chelsea, Real Madrid, FC Barcelona, Paris Saint-Germain, Juventus, Bayern Munich, Borussia Dortmund – has increased from 22% to 39% of the combined sum of the incomes of the participants in the main European leagues, whereas nearly half (49%) of total income is generated by the 30 wealthiest European clubs. It must be mentioned, however, that in that period the incomes of European clubs have increased overall from 11.4 billion to 20.1 billion euro (UEFA, 2019).

Scholars also differ in their opinions regarding the effects of the changes carried out in business models in terms of their structure and sources of financing. Even before the UEFA regulation was implemented, in a study of the financial data from annual reports for the period 2001–2010, Wilson et al. (2013) noted that the financial models of football clubs floated on the stock market were more often aligned with FFP rules. These clubs were also in a better financial condition than clubs funded from domestic resources or by foreign private investors. Nevertheless, studies have shown that the source of capital is important in such cases. Clubs owned by foreign investors achieved better sports results compared to clubs funded by domestic sponsors. These studies have also revealed that clubs pursuing a short-term maximisation of sports results depend on substantial investments, particularly from foreign investors. Szymański (2012), however, heavily criticised the restrictions FFP placed on club funding, citing conclusions drawn from studies on the English league, which suggest that the poor financial situation of a club is not necessarily a consequence of the wasteful spending of its owners and excessive contributions meant to satisfy the ambition of achieving a better position in the league, but is the result of independent external events which cause a decrease in productivity or affect demand (e.g. injuries, bad luck on the field, decreased value of media contracts). Nonetheless, Franck (2014) stresses that FFP in fact only limits owners in terms of payments for salaries, while investments unrelated to payrolls remain unregulated. This creates the opportunity to invest resources in infrastructure, social projects and youth academies, which in turn generate potential future sources of revenue from young players, increased supporter turnout, or sponsorship contracts. A UEFA report published in 2019 indicates that FFP had a strong impact on club balance sheets in terms of changing the level and structure of liabilities. Owner contributions and capital increases during the period 2008–2017 increased by nearly 12 billion euros, while net equity (assets minus debts and liabilities) increased to 7.7 billion euros (from 1.9 billion in 2008) (UEFA, 2019).

Another effect attributed to FFP is the limitation of serious losses. In the 2017 fiscal year, clubs generated a total profit of 615 million euros for the first time (UEFA, 2019). Moreover, the report shows that recent years have seen a stable trend of revenue increase compared to expenses. During their studies of the Italian league, Nicoliello and Zampatti (2016) confirmed that the key factors affecting profits are located within expenses. The most crucial among them are player wages. The basic revenue of clubs comes from the net profit from player transfers. Other revenue sources, such as broadcasting rights or advertising revenue are not statistically relevant in profit generation (Nicoliello and Zampatti, 2016). However, it must be noted that in general, the revenue from the sale of broadcasting rights increased by 113% over the period 2008–2017 and a very important part of the budgets of clubs from less wealthy leagues – bonuses received from UEFA – increased by 228% (UEFA, 2019). However, the studies of Ghio et al. (2019), which were based on data from the period 2005–2015, show that FFP did not improve the average performance of Italian first-league clubs. Additionally, the research suggests that FFP has contributed to narrowing the performance gap between teams at the highest and lowest sports levels. Furthermore, based on their own findings, Gallagher and Quinn (2019) claimed that the break-even point regulations decrease the overall sports and financial effectiveness of clubs, with the performance loss positively related to the severity of the break-even point restriction.

On the basis of the UEFA report, it could also be said that a heightened activity on the transfer market was observable in the period 2012–2017, resulting in ever higher sums of money being offered for football players. Previously, Peeters and Szymanski (2014) had warned that the UEFA regulation would considerably restrict competition on the player market and place greater pressure on lowering wages, without improving competitive balance, and Madden (2012) had argued that assuming a relatively high elasticity in the supply of talent in the league, FFP regulation diminishes value for the players, owners, and supporters alike. As noted by Dimitropoulos and Scafarto (2019) in their studies of Italian clubs based on data from the period 2007–2017, FFP altered clubs' business models over the years: from a concept oriented towards investments (spending on wages) to an efficiency model focused on deriving profits from player trading. The researchers suggest that, because of this, club managers should concentrate on creating permanent player transfer cycles in order to evolve in the environment of new regulations. According to this research, FFP leads to more efficient decision-making regarding player transfers and consequently has a positive effect on the relation between profit from player transfers and financial results (Dimitropoulos and Scafarto, 2019).

The main purpose of this chapter is to identify the effects of the modifications introduced in business models under FFP rules, in terms of:

- sources of revenue,
- models of funding of the activity,
- levels and structures of key resources,
- levels of cost-effectiveness,
- levels of profitability.

## Materials and methods

In order to achieve the established goal, it is necessary to analyse indicators around the financial data of clubs pertaining to particular areas of the business model. Our research sample consists of the top 50 European football clubs, according to the 2017 UEFA ranking. This ranking was chosen because it includes points over a period of five years, covering the period in which FFP came into effect. In the process of gathering financial data, it was possible to initially select approximately 30 clubs with available data. A subsequent verification of this data has ultimately reduced this number to 27 clubs, but not for all analyses. For some analyses it was possible to use data from only 24 or 26 football clubs. The data was gathered for the period 2012–2017 in order to have a reporting period of at least three years for each club included in the research. The chosen time frame made it possible to analyse how the business models of European clubs have changed during the period when FFP came into effect. In order to assess changes in sources of revenue acquisition, four basic groups of revenue were classified: merchandising revenue, TV broadcasting, match day, and other. That classification is the most common in research literature, and the revenue data from club sales is often divided in this manner. A debt ratio indicator was used to evaluate the funding structure, calculated as total liabilities divided by total assets. This indicator is also complementary in evaluating liquidity, and is one of the indicators used in FFP regulations (UEFA, 2019). A non-current assets in total assets ratio indicator was used to evaluate the resource structure. The data gathered has allowed only a limited analysis, and was not adequate for a detailed review of the components of club assets. In the case of cost-effectiveness, salaries are of key importance, as pointed out by other researchers (Dimitropoulos and Scafarto, 2019; Franck, 2014; Hamil and Walters, 2010; Peeters and Szymanski, 2014). For this reason, the adopted indicator for salary efficiency is the ratio of salaries to sales revenue. The changes in the final area of the business model were measured by gross profit due its comparability between different formats of collected data and to avoid the fiscal differences between countries. Nevertheless, it must be remembered that profitability is not one the primary objectives of sports clubs. Sánchez et al. (2017) have noticed that a large number of club owners does not seek monetary compensation for their investments, therefore there is no point in considering profitability as an indicator of investment utility. The authors suggest substituting it with a coefficient of efficiency as a measure of investment utility that takes into account the degree to which the different objectives of the owner have been achieved, including sports success. Measures of descriptive statistics were used in the analyses, such as arithmetic mean, median, and variance coefficient. For the detailed data about the selected clubs, positive changes in a given area of the business model were marked with a value of "1". In the case of no positive changes in a given area, the clubs were marked with a value of "0".

## Results

The first area of the business model is the sales revenue structure. Analysing this structure provides a basis for assessing the type and extent of the changes that took place within the duration of FFP.

Figure 5.1 illustrates the change in the revenue structure that occurred under FFP. Cumulative data shows an increased share of merchandising revenue at the expense of TV broadcasting share. One of the motives for FFP was to draw the attention of club managers to the necessity of increasing revenue from sources other than TV broadcasting, whose previously very large share posed a risk to clubs, and in the case of the English league served as one of the causes of player salary inflation (Perechuda, 2019). A detailed analysis of the change of revenue diversification has been carried out and presented in Table 5.2.

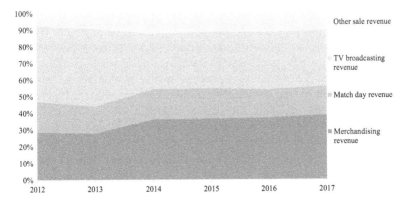

*Figure 5.1* Revenue diversification in the total sample.

*Table 5.2* Revenue – changes (increase or decrease) of coefficient of variation

| | Median of coefficient of variation change | Mean of coefficient of variation change | Positive change measured by median | Positive change measured by mean |
|---|---|---|---|---|
| AC Milan | −8% | −6% | 1 | 1 |
| AS Monaco | 42% | 42% | 0 | 0 |
| Athletico M | 3% | 4% | 0 | 0 |
| Bay Munch | −1% | 0% | 1 | 0 |
| BCN | 1% | 2% | 0 | 0 |
| Borussia MG | 3% | 4% | 0 | 0 |
| BVB | 2% | 3% | 0 | 0 |
| Chelsea | 5% | 5% | 0 | 0 |
| FC Basel | 2% | 3% | 0 | 0 |
| Fiorentina | 14% | 9% | 0 | 0 |
| Juve | −3% | −2% | 1 | 1 |
| Lazio | 3% | 6% | 0 | 0 |
| Liverpool | −1% | −1% | 1 | 1 |
| Malaga | −9% | −9% | 1 | 1 |
| ManCity | 0% | 0% | 1 | 0 |
| MANU | 6% | 5% | 0 | 0 |
| Olimp_Pir | 12% | 12% | 0 | 0 |
| Porto | −9% | 1% | 1 | 0 |
| PSG | −6% | −11% | 1 | 1 |
| Real M | −8% | −28% | 1 | 1 |
| Roma | 5% | 5% | 0 | 0 |
| Schalke | 2% | 2% | 0 | 0 |
| Sporting | −8% | −6% | 1 | 1 |
| Tottenham | 16% | 12% | 0 | 0 |
| Valencia | 8% | 8% | 0 | 0 |
| Wolfsburg | −1% | 0% | 1 | 0 |
| | | | 11 of 26 | 7 of 26 |

In order to perform a detailed verification of the process of revenue diversification, it was necessary to measure the changes of the variance coefficient. The measuring process involved calculating the variance coefficient for the values of particular revenue sources from one year, followed by verifying the change (increase or decrease) of the variance coefficient over the years in a given club. This analysis enables an answer to the question of whether the revenue diversification has improved in a club on average (i.e. the revenues were more evenly distributed). The analysis also shows that in the case of a mean value of change, seven out of 26 clubs have improved their structure, and when applying the median value of change the number of such clubs is 11. The research concerns improving the situation of revenue diversification from year to year. An in-depth analysis does not indicate improvement in the situation of most clubs, in contrast to what can be observed in Figure 5.1.

The next business model area which was examined is sources of funding of clubs (Figure 5.2).

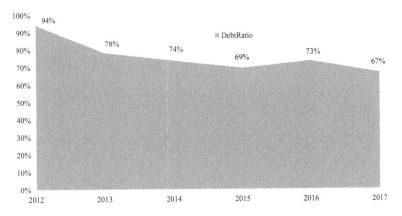

*Figure 5.2*  Debt ratio in the total sample.

Debt ratio was chosen for the analysis of funding sources, which led to an observation that, during the research period, all of the clubs exhibited a decrease in debt, and consequently a larger share of equity funding. The improvement of this ratio is one of the key effects of implementing FFP (Table 5.3).

An in-depth analysis of each club has demonstrated that the debt ratio has improved in 12 out of 24 analysed cases when the average change was measured by the median, and in 15 out of 24 cases when the change was measured by the arithmetic mean. Regarding sources of funding, it can be said that while FFP was in force the majority of clubs decreased their debt to levels below 70% indebtedness. Additionally, in contrast to the analysis of revenue diversification, debt improvement occurred in at least half of the investigated clubs. In the following step, the asset structure of clubs was analysed in order to determine what changes occurred in club resources. Unfortunately, the data gathered was not detailed enough to specify the most significant asset positions precisely. This analysis is based only on studying the change between non-current assets and total assets (Figure 5.3).

Examining the sum of gathered data, it is possible to observe a systematic increase in the share of non-current assets in the asset

*Table 5.3* Debt ratio changes

| TL/TA | Median of change | Mean of change | Positive change measured by median | Positive change measured by mean |
|---|---|---|---|---|
| AC Milan | 2.2% | −0.1% | 0 | 1 |
| AS Monaco | 0.1% | 0.6% | 0 | 0 |
| Athletico M | 0.1% | 0.3% | 0 | 0 |
| Bay Munch | −4.1% | −4.4% | 1 | 1 |
| BCN | −3.5% | −3.2% | 1 | 1 |
| Borussia MG | 0.6% | 0.6% | 0 | 0 |
| BVB | −1.1% | −4.7% | 1 | 1 |
| Chelsea | −3.1% | 4.0% | 1 | 0 |
| Fiorentina | 0.3% | −0.1% | 0 | 1 |
| Juve | −0.3% | 0.0% | 1 | 1 |
| Liverpool | −6.3% | −14.3% | 1 | 1 |
| Malaga | 29.7% | 29.7% | 0 | 0 |
| ManCity | 0.9% | 0.8% | 0 | 0 |
| MANU | 2.4% | 2.2% | 0 | 0 |
| Olimp_Pir | −3.7% | −3.4% | 1 | 1 |
| Porto | 12.5% | 5.4% | 0 | 0 |
| PSG | −1.7% | −0.9% | 1 | 1 |
| PSV Eind | −2.2% | −1.7% | 1 | 1 |
| Real M | 3.7% | −0.8% | 0 | 1 |
| Roma | −1.9% | −4.4% | 1 | 1 |
| Schalke_new | −10.0% | −8.4% | 1 | 1 |
| Sporting | 2.2% | −0.1% | 0 | 1 |
| Valencia | 2.0% | −0.8% | 0 | 1 |
| Wolfsburg | −1.9% | 0.3% | 1 | 0 |
| | | | 12 of 24 | 15 of 24 |

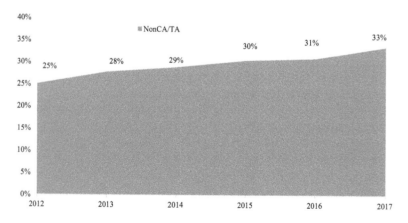

*Figure 5.3* Non-current assets in total assets ratio in the total sample.

structure. This situation can also be considered as a negative change in club resources. This change means that the share of current assets of clubs is becoming progressively smaller and in consequence, their liquidity may become limited. Comparing this information with the decreasing indebtedness of clubs (Figure 5.2), it can be surmised that current assets will be reduced due to lower liabilities. This research is limited by the lack of information concerning the structure of liabilities. Future studies may answer the question of whether short-term liabilities are also limited in a given time frame, and only at that time will it be possible to determine whether the liquidity of clubs is improving or worsening. The asset analysis of clubs also suggests that non-current assets, including purchased players and club infrastructure such as stadiums, have increased over time. It can be assumed that, under FFP, clubs have been investing in their resources.

Players are one of the key resources of clubs and the key measure of the efficiency of this resource is the ratio of salaries to club revenue (Dimitropoulos and Scafarto, 2019; Perechuda, 2019).

After analysing Figure 5.4, it can be observed that in the chosen total sample there is a decrease of S/R ratio below 60%, but after that the ratio is stable. It also confirms what was observed by Perechuda (2019), that S/R ratio in the clubs with the best sports performance is between 50% and approximately 60% (Table 5.4).

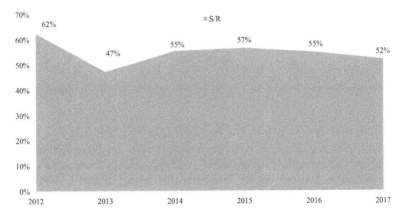

*Figure 5.4* Salaries/revenues ratio in the total sample.

An improvement of the situation in over half of the studied cases is observed in the detailed analysis, regardless of whether the improvement was measured by median (18 out of 27) or by arithmetical mean (16 out of 27). This also complements the conclusions drawn in previous

*Table 5.4* Salaries/revenues ratio changes

| | Median of change | Mean of change | Positive change measured by median | Positive change measured by mean |
|---|---|---|---|---|
| AC Milan | −0.3% | 0.7% | 1 | 0 |
| AS Monaco | −47.9% | −47.9% | 1 | 1 |
| Athletico M | −3.8% | −2.3% | 1 | 1 |
| Bay Munch | −0.8% | −0.9% | 1 | 1 |
| BCN | 4.3% | 0.2% | 0 | 0 |
| Borussia MG | −3.8% | −2.3% | 1 | 1 |
| BVB | 2.5% | 2.9% | 0 | 0 |
| Chelsea | −1.1% | −1.4% | 1 | 1 |
| FC Basel | 3.1% | 2.9% | 0 | 0 |
| Fiorentina | −2.1% | 0.6% | 1 | 0 |
| Juve | 1.2% | 0.9% | 0 | 0 |
| Lazio | −1.7% | −0.5% | 1 | 1 |
| Liverpool | −3.9% | −1.6% | 1 | 1 |
| Malaga | −12.5% | −12.5% | 1 | 1 |
| ManCity | −4.3% | −7.6% | 1 | 1 |
| MANU | 0.1% | −1.1% | 0 | 1 |
| Olimp_Pir | −6.3% | −6.5% | 1 | 1 |
| Porto | 6.1% | 9.0% | 0 | 0 |
| PSG | 0.7% | −0.2% | 0 | 1 |
| PSV Eind | −5.4% | −2.2% | 1 | 1 |
| Real M | −1.1% | −0.5% | 1 | 1 |
| Roma | 1.7% | 1.8% | 0 | 0 |
| Schalke_new | −1.0% | 0.2% | 1 | 0 |
| Sporting | −0.3% | 0.7% | 1 | 0 |
| Tottenham | −5.3% | −5.9% | 1 | 1 |
| Valencia | 10.3% | 5.8% | 0 | 0 |
| Wolfsburg | −0.8% | −0.9% | 1 | 1 |
| | | | 18 of 27 | 16 of 27 |

research, that the clubs with the best sports results (the studied clubs belong to the top 50 of the UEFA ranking) maintain their S/R ratio below the average value, i.e. below 62%. Moreover, the average of this ratio in this study does not deviate from the average derived by Perechuda (2019). The final analysed business model area is revenue profitability. In order for this analysis to be proportional, the examined value is gross income, which does not include the tax burden (Figure 5.5).

In the total sample, a systematic increase of gross revenue margin from 2.9% to 5.1% can be observed, except for a decrease in 2014. As long as the aim of FFP was to increase the stability of profits in football clubs, it is apparent that it succeeded in the total sample. The research of Nicoliello and Zampatti (2016) showed that the improvement of profitability depends on the wage policies of clubs. Our findings confirm this. In the research period, the S/R ratio has improved, as well as profitability in a global perspective (Table 5.5).

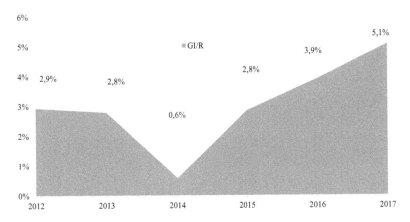

*Figure 5.5* Gross revenue margin in the total sample.

It is specifically observable that the improvement of profitability in the research period was exhibited on average in 17 out of 27 clubs (measured by median) or in 13 out of 27 clubs (measured by arithmetical mean). This constitutes the majority of studied clubs. The majority of researched clubs have also improved the cost-efficiency of salaries, which is the justification for regarding salaries as key expenses in football clubs. It is also worth mentioning that an average of 18 out of 27 clubs exhibited a positive gross result, which constitutes more than half of the clubs in the research.

## Conclusions

In general, many researchers argue that FFP has put great emphasis on management quality. Egon Franck (2014) points out the effectiveness of the solutions implemented, particularly in the enforcement of hard budget constraints. A similar conclusion, based on the study of Italian clubs, was reached by Dimitropoulos and Scafarto (2019), namely that FFP restored effective managerial incentives in football businesses, which, in fact, is an argument for full implementation of the regulations. On the other hand, Szymański (2012) argues that by focusing on managerial faults, FFP overlooks the actual causes of insolvency. In the course of this research, it has been noted that the

*Table 5.5* Gross margin ratio changes

| | Gross margin mean | Positive margin in studied period | Median of change | Mean of change | Positive change measured by median | Positive change measured by mean |
|---|---|---|---|---|---|---|
| AC Milan | −24.4% | 0 | −5.2% | −7.9% | 0 | 0 |
| AS Monaco | −15.5% | 0 | −20.7% | −20.7% | 0 | 0 |
| Athletico M | 2.6% | 1 | 0.6% | 0.1% | 1 | 1 |
| Bay Munch | 6.5% | 1 | 0.9% | 1.0% | 1 | 1 |
| BCN | 6.8% | 1 | 0.7% | −1.0% | 1 | 0 |
| Borussia MG | 2.8% | 1 | 0.2% | −0.1% | 1 | 0 |
| BVB | 9.4% | 1 | −6.5% | −5.3% | 0 | 0 |
| Chelsea | 11.6% | 1 | −6.5% | −3.9% | 0 | 0 |
| FC Basel | 9.4% | 1 | −6.5% | −5.3% | 0 | 0 |
| Fiorentina | −11.5% | 0 | 9.5% | −0.3% | 1 | 0 |
| Juve | 3.4% | 1 | 3.7% | 4.6% | 1 | 1 |
| Lazio | 2.1% | 1 | 7.9% | 5.2% | 1 | 1 |
| Liverpool | 0.1% | 1 | 18.5% | 8.8% | 1 | 1 |
| Malaga | −3.1% | 0 | 3.8% | 3.8% | 1 | 1 |
| ManCity | 6.7% | 1 | −4.3% | −4.8% | 0 | 0 |
| MANU | 5.0% | 1 | 5.3% | 3.0% | 1 | 1 |
| Olimp_Pir | −0.7% | 0 | −3.9% | −2.6% | 0 | 0 |
| Porto | −25.7% | 0 | −26.3% | −19.1% | 0 | 0 |
| PSG | −0.1% | 0 | 0.1% | −0.8% | 1 | 0 |
| PSV Eind | 3.4% | 1 | 0.1% | 0.7% | 1 | 1 |
| Real M | 7.5% | 1 | 0.3% | 0.0% | 1 | 0 |
| Roma | −20.2% | 0 | 4.4% | 2.2% | 1 | 1 |
| Schalke_new | 5.6% | 1 | 4.8% | 5.3% | 1 | 1 |
| Sporting | −24.4% | 0 | −5.2% | −7.9% | 0 | 0 |
| Tottenham | 18.0% | 1 | 6.4% | 4.1% | 1 | 1 |
| Valencia | 11.6% | 1 | −2.1% | 2.1% | 0 | 1 |
| Wolfsburg | 6.5% | 1 | 0.9% | 1.0% | 1 | 1 |
| | | 18 of 27 | | | 17 of 27 | 13 of 27 |

share of merchandising revenue in the business models of football clubs has increased, decreasing the dependence of clubs on TV broadcasting. Detailed analysis, on the other hand, has shown that a positive change in the revenue structure of business models has occurred only in the minority of investigated clubs. This corresponds with the results of previous research on the effects of FFP, which stated that implementing these regulations would only render the competition less flexible, and any positive changes would occur in clubs which were already in a favourable business situation (Birkhäuser et al., 2019). The changes observed in the resource structure and in the effectiveness of salaries are supportive of previous research. Dimitropoulos and Scafarto (2019) suggested that FFP drove a shift in the business model of Italian clubs from being investment focused (wage spending) to more efficiency-driven, which relied (to a greater extent than before) on player trading. In our research we can see that the S/R ratio was reduced, and at the same time we observed an increase in non-current assets share in total assets, which could confirm the change in business model towards increasing the value of players which was disclosed in the balance sheet. FFP also had positive impact on the profitability of clubs, which has improved in the research period both globally and in counting the number of clubs. The explanation for this situation should be sought in the wage policy of clubs, which has adapted to the new regulations.

It is undeniable that changes have occurred in the business models of the chosen clubs during the time of FFP. Moreover, the changes observed in this paper partially confirm the findings of other scholars. Nevertheless, it cannot be said that the observed positive changes involve a clear majority of researched clubs. Depending on the business model area, positive changes affected roughly half of the studied cases. This may be a result of what has been noted before, that FFP strengthened the business and sports positions of clubs which were already performing well in a sports and business sense. It can be confidently asserted that FFP has changed business models, but it cannot be said that the business models in the majority of cases have improved overall. It is apparent that the majority of clubs were unable to improve the diversification of their revenue. What has improved, however, is funding and the cost-efficiency of salaries.

## Bibliography

Adner, R., Kapoor, R. (2010). Value creation in innovation ecosystems: How the structure of technological interdependence affects firm performance in new technology generations. *Strategic Management Journal*, 31(3): 306–333.

Amit, R, Zott, C. (2001). Value creation in e-business. *Strategic Management Journal,* 22(6/7): 493–520.

Amit, R., Zott, C. (2012). Creating value through business model innovation. *MIT Sloan Management Review*, 53: 41–49.

Amit, R., Zott, C. (2015). Crafting business architecture: The antecedents of business model design. *Strategic Entrepreneurship Journal*, 9(4): 331–350.

Andries, P., Debackere, K. (2007). Adaptation and performance in new businesses: Understanding the moderating effects of independence and industry. *Small Business Economics,* 29(1/2): 81–99.

Anthony, S. (2012). The new corporate garage. *Harvard Business Review*, 9: 44–53.

Baden-Fuller, C., Haefliger, S. (2013). Business models and technological innovation. *Long Range Planning*, 46: 419–426.

Barajas, A., Rodríguez, P. (2010). Spanish football clubs' finances: Crisis and player salaries. *International Journal of Sport Finance*, 5 (1): 52.

Birkhäuser, S., Kaserer C., Urban, D. (2019). Did UEFA's financial fair play harm competition in European football leagues? *Review of Managerial Science*, 13(1): 113–145. doi:10.1007/s11846-017-0246-z

Brea-Solís, H., Casadesus-Masanell, R., Grifell-Tatje, E. (2015) Business model evaluation: Quantifying Walmart's sources of advantage. *Strategic Entrepreneurship Journal*, 9: 12–33.

Casadesus-Masanell, R., Ricart, J.E. (2010). From strategy to business models and to tactics. *Long Range Planning*, 43: 195–215.

Casadesus-Masanell, R., Ricart, J.E. (2011). How to design a winning business model. *Harvard Business Review*, 89: 100–107.

Chesbrough, H., Rosenbloom, R.S. (2002). The role of the business model in capturing value from innovation: Evidence from Xerox Corporation's technology spin-off companies. *Industrial and Corporate Change,* 11: 529–555.

De Reuver, M., Bouwman, H., MacInnes, I. (2009). Business models dynamics for start-ups and innovating e-businesses. *International Journal of Electronic Business*, 7: 269–286.

Demil, B., Lecocq, X., Ricart, J., Zott, C. (2015). Introduction to the SEJ special issue on business models: Business models within the domain of strategic entrepreneurship. *Strategic Entrepreneurship Journal*, 9(1): 1–11. https://doi.org/10.1002/sej.1194

Dimitropoulos, P. E., & Tsagkanos, A. (2012). Financial Performance and Corporate Governance in the European Football Industry. *International Journal of Sport Finance*, 7(4).

Dimitropoulos, P. (2016). Audit selection in the European football industry under Union of European Football Associations financial fair play. *International Journal of Economics and Financial Issues*, 6(3): 901–906.

Dimitropoulos, P., Scafarto, V. (2019). The impact of UEFA financial fair play on player expenditures, sporting success and financial performance: Evidence from the Italian top league. *European Sport Management Quarterly*. doi:10.1080/16184742.2019.1674896

Drut, B., & Raballand, G. (2012). Why does financial regulation matter for European professional football clubs?. *International Journal of Sport Management and Marketing* 2, 11(1–2), 73–88.

Doz, Y. L., Kosonen, M. (2010). Embedding strategic agility: A leadership agenda for accelerating business model renewal. *Long Range Planning*, 43: 370–382.

Franck, E. P. (2014). Financial Fair Play in European club football-what is it all about?. *University of Zurich, Department of Business Administration, UZH Business Working Paper*, 328.

Einolf, K. W. (2004). Is winning everything? A data envelopment analysis of Major League Baseball and the National Football League. *Journal of Sports Economics*, 5(2): 127–151.

Ferreira, F. N. H., Proença, J. F., Spencer, R., Cova, B. (2013). The transition from products to solutions: External business model fit and dynamics. *Industrial Marketing Management*, 42(7): 1093–1101.

Foss, N. J., Saebi, T. (2017). Fifteen years of research on business model innovation: How far have we come, and where should we go? *Journal of Management*, 43: 200–227. doi:10.1177/0149206316675927

Galariotis, E., Germain, C., Zopounidis, C. (2018). A combined methodology for the concurrent evaluation of the business, financial and sports performance of football clubs: The case of France. *Annals of Operations Research*, 266(1–2): 589–612.

Gallagher, R., Quinn, B. (2019). Regulatory own goals: The unintended consequences of economic regulation in professional football. *European Sport Management Quarterly*. doi:10.1080/16184742.2019.1588344

Ghio, A., Ruberti, M., Verona, R. (2019). Financial constraints on sport organizations' cost efficiency: The impact of financial fair play on Italian soccer clubs. *Applied Economics*, 51(24): 2623–2638. doi:10.1080/00036846.2018.1558348

Hamil, S., Walters, G. (2010). Financial performance in English professional football: 'An inconvenient truth'. *Soccer & Society*, 11(4): 354–372. doi:10.1080/14660971003780214

Johnson, M. W., Christensen, C. M., Kagermann, H. (2008). Reinventing your business model. *Harvard Business Review*, 86(12): 50–59.

Joyce, A., Paquin, R. L. (2016). The triple layered business model canvas: a tool to design more sustainable business models. *Journal of Cleaner Production*, 135: 1474–1486.

Madden, P. (2012). Welfare economics of "financial fair play" in a sports league with benefactor owners. *Journal of Sports Economics*, 16(2): 159–184. doi:10.1177/1527002512465759

Markides, C. (2006). Disruptive innovation: In need of better theory. *Journal of Product Innovation Management*, 23: 19–25.

Massa, L., Tucci, C., Afuah, A. (2017). A critical assessment of business model research. *Academy of Management Annals*, 11(1): 73–104.

McGrath, R. G. (2010). Business models: A discovery-driven approach. *Long Range Planning*, 43: 247–261.

Menary, S. (2016). One rule for one: The impact of champions league prize money and financial fair play at the bottom of the European club game. *Soccer and Society*, 17(5): 666–679. doi:10.1080/14660970.2015.1103073

Mitchell, D., Coles, C. (2003). The ultimate competitive advantage of continuing business model innovation. *Journal of Business Strategy*, 24(5): 15–21.

Morrow, S. (2013). Football club financial reporting: Time for a new model? *Sport, Business and Management: An International Journal*, 3(4): 297–311. doi:10.1108/SBM-06-2013-0014.

Müller, J. C., Lammert, J., & Hovemann, G. (2012). The financial fair play regulations of UEFA: an adequate concept to ensure the long-term viability and sustainability of European club football?. *International Journal of Sport Finance*, 7(2).

Nicoliello, M., Zampatti, D. (2016). Football clubs' profitability after the financial fair play regulation: Evidence from Italy. *Sport, Business and Management: An International Journal*, 6(4): 460–475. doi:10.1108/SBM-07-2014-0037.

Osterwalder, A., Pigneur, Y. (2010). *Business model generation: A Handbook for visionaries, game changers, and challengers.* Hoboken, NJ: Wiley.

Osterwalder, A., Pigneur, Y., Tucci, C. L. (2005). Clarifying business models: Origins, present, and future of the concept. *Communications of the Association for Information Systems*, 16: 1–25.

Peeters, T., Szymanski, S. (2014). Financial fair play in European football. *Economic Policy*, 29: 343–390.

Perechuda, I. (2019). Salaries to revenue ratio efficiency in football clubs in Europe. In: Bilgin M., Danis H., Demir E., Can U. (eds), *Eurasian economic perspectives. Eurasian studies in business and economics* (vol. 10/2, pp. 301–314). Cham: Springer.

Ramchandani, G. (2012). Competitiveness of the English Premier League (1992-2010) and ten European football leagues (2010). *International Journal of Performance Analysis in Sport*, 12(2), 346–360.

Sabatier, V., Craig-Kennard, A., Mangematin, V. (2012). When technological discontinuities and disruptive business models challenge dominant industry logics: Insights from the drugs industry. *Technological Forecasting and Social Change*, 79: 946–962.

Saebi, T., Lien, L., Foss, N. J. (2016). What drives business model adaption? The impact of opportunities, threats and strategic orientation. *Long Range Planning*, 50(5): 567–581.

Sánchez, L. C., Barajas, Á., Sánchez-Fernández, P. (2017). Does the agency theory play football? *Universia Business Review*, 53: 18–59.

Sánchez, L. C., Barajas, Á., Sánchez-Fernández, P. (2020). Profits may lead teams to lose matches, but scoring goals does not lead to profit. *European Research on Management and Business Economics*, 26: 26–32.

Sass, M. (2012). Long-term competitive balance under UEFA financial fair play regulations. FEMM Working Papers No. 5/2012. Otto-von-Guericke University Magdeburg, Faculty of Economics and Management, Magdeburg.

Sass, M. (2016). Glory hunters, sugar daddies, and long-term competitive balance under UEFA financial fair play. *Journal of Sports Economics*, 17(2): 148–158. doi:10.1177/1527002514526412

Scelles, N., Dermit-Richard, N., Haynes, R. (2019). What drives sports TV rights? A comparative analysis of their evolution in English and French men's football first divisions, 1980–2020. *Soccer & Society,* 21(5): 1–19.

Sims, P. J. (2018). The circumvention of UEFA's financial fair play rules through the influx of foreign investments. *Northwestern Journal of International Law and Business*, 39(1): 59–84.

Solberg, H. A., Haugen, K. K. (2010). European club football: Why enormous revenues are not enough? *Sport in Society*, 13(2), 329–343. doi:10.1080/17430430903523036.

Szymanski, S. (2012). Insolvency in English professional football: Irrational exuberance or negative shocks? *Working Paper No. 12-02*. North American Association of Sport Economics.

Szymanski, S. (2014). Fair is foul: A critical analysis of UEFA financial fair play. *International Journal of Sport Finance*, 9: 218–229.

Schubert, M., & Könecke, T. (2015). 'Classical' doping, financial doping and beyond: UEFA's financial fair play as a policy of anti-doping. *International Journal of Sport Policy and Politics*, 7(1), 63–86.

Szymanski, S. (2017). Entry into exit: Insolvency in English professional football. *Scottish Journal of Political Economy*, 64(4): 419–444.

Teece, D. J. (2010). Business models, business strategy and innovation. *Long Range Planning*, 43: 172–194.

UEFA. (2012). *Financial fair play and club licensing regulations* (2012 edition). Nyon: UEFA.

UEFA. (2019). *Club licensing benchmarking report financial year 2017.* Nyon: UEFA.

Vöpel, H. (2011). Do we really need financial fair play in European club football? An economic analysis. *CESifo DICE Report*, 9(3): 54–59.

Vrooman, J. (1997). A unified theory of capital and labour markets in major league baseball. *Southern Economic Journal,* 63: 594–619.

Weill, P., Woerner, S. L. (2013). Optimizing your digital business model. *MIT Sloan Management Review*, 54(2): 71–78.

Wessel, M., Levie, A., Siegel, R. (2016). Legacy ecosystems: They separate you from your customer. *Harvard Business Review*, 94(11): 68–74.

Wilson, R., Plumley, D., Ramchandani, G. (2013). The relationship between ownership structure and club performance in the English premier league. *Sport, Business and Management: An International Journal*, 3(1): 19–36. doi:10.1108/20426781311316889

Wirtz, B. W., Pistoia, A., Ullrich, S., Göttel, V. (2016). Business models: Origin, development and future research perspectives. *Long Range Planning*, 49: 36–54.

Zollo, M., Cennamo, C., Neumann, K. (2013). Beyond what and why: Understanding organizational evolution towards sustainable enterprise models. *Organization and Environment*, 26: 241–259.

# 6 The Role of Payment Services and Wearable Devices in Amateur Sport

*Mikołaj Borowski-Beszta and Michał Polasik*

## Introduction

With the development of technology in sport, the role of measurement of training and body parameters, especially in real-time, is increasing. Amateur sport has different characteristics when compared to professionals, as the training takes place independently, without the support of a coach or specialised equipment, often in an open field. The amateur sportsperson in training is mostly on their own, without access to financial services. The development of cheap, wearable devices has a crucial role for sports amateurs. Due to wearables' high availability in retail stores, such users can monitor their progress, body parameters, and life balance, as well as purchase goods needed for training (i.e. water) without effort (Borowski-Beszta & Polasik, 2020). The functions of various digital wearables and smartphones constitute a virtual trainer. At the same time, manufacturers meet the needs of users for whom carrying a smartphone or wallet during training is a problem, as payments are a feature that appears more and more often in devices of this type. Continuous improvements make wearable payments easy, with guaranteed security as well as independence during training sessions. In some of the circumstances outlined above, the fact that wearable devices do not require constant integration with a smartphone might also be significant.

Despite the growing number of users and applications of wearable devices among sports amateurs, this has not so far been the subject of extensive research in Poland. The data presented in this chapter is among the first regarding payment contexts in wearables in both quantitative and qualitative research.

The main aim of this research is to investigate the role of innovative payment-enabled wearables in amateur sport. As part of the work, the authors strive to provide an in-depth analysis of selected aspects of the

DOI: 10.4324/9781003270126-7

use of payment and health-monitoring functionalities as well as the causes and motivations for usage. The chapter briefly explains the definition and use of wearable devices and discusses the development of the wearables market in the world in terms of direction and dynamics, providing a full view of the wearable market.

The main part of work is based on two types of empirical research. The first is an online CAWI survey that enables quantification of the coverage of the wearables market and shows the extent of use of wearables devices and digital payments. The second type of data is qualitative, enabling comparison of the use of wearables as well as in-depth understanding of the motives for usage by users who participate in amateur sports alongside a control group that is not involved in sports. The research produces findings that are essential in the context of sport digitisation and may point to some crucial tips for producers of this type of equipment, as well as for organisers of sporting events such as marathons and other mass events.

## Specifics of wearables

Wearables are a specific type of electronic device that the user can wear on the body. They can be smartwatches, smart bands, smart glasses, smart jewellery or any other accessories that collect user data (Chuah et al., 2016). As pointed out by Tarabasz and Poddar (2019), wearable devices include a far greater variety than those listed above. For instance, they can also include items like clothing and the definition also applies to electronic devices that "can be comfortably worn around the body." The first devices of this type appeared back in the twentieth century (Thorp, 1998) but significant developments of the wearable market started around 2006. The major breakthrough took place in 2014, when the first Apple Watch was introduced (Borowski-Beszta & Polasik, 2020). Devices of this type provide the user with both power and flexibility as they are filled with a variety of sensors that provide the key framework for a more in-depth approach to personal health monitoring (Kheirkhahan et al., 2019). Modern devices of this type allow both physical data (Guk et al., 2019) and psychological analysis (Ollander, Godin, Campagne, & Charbonnier, 2017). Heartbeat pattern recording, sleep and exercise patterns might be considered as the standard health-monitoring functionalities of wearables (Yildirim & Ali-Eldin, 2019). When used in conjunction with data such as time, the information collected about pulse or distance travelled becomes essential for athletes, giving them reference data from which to manage their training sessions and health (Wang, 2015). At the same time, wrist-worn wearables are a hub that combines health and sports with other value-added services, such as messaging, weather, GPS or even a web browser. They are considered as mini-computers providing numerous functions (Chuah et al., 2016) and are a touchpoint between vital technological trends: mobile technologies, the Internet of Things (IoT), Augmented Reality (AR) and Big Data (Tarabasz & Poddar, 2019).

## Mobile platforms as a complementary tool to wearable devices

The pivotal tools for managing data obtained from wearables are various types of sports platforms and mobile applications. They include, among others, Strava, Peloton Cycle or one of the oldest, the Endomondo platform created in 2007, withdrawn in January 2021. These applications are often a kind of activity diary and help monitor various parameters, such as the number of steps taken or the distance covered during a walk, or in running or cycling. Apps often have different publishers and are tailored to the respective sporting activities. They are both a positive incentive and a self-efficacy booster (Lim & Noh, 2017). For many users, sports platforms are a highly valued and integral part of sports activities (Rivers, 2019). Sports applications are very popular these days. Manufacturers of sports footwear also have their own sports applications, including Adidas Running by Runtastic or Nike Run Club (Google Play, 2021). Sports applications enable the promotion of various social campaigns. One of them was the annual T-Mobile telecom campaign which operated in Poland in 2013–2019 – the distance travelled by users of the sports application was converted into funds, which were transferred to social foundations and children with disabilities (T-Mobile, 2021).

Sports applications and platforms also enable social research. It is worth mentioning the research carried out by Tison et al. (2020). Using the Argus application (by Azumio), the impact of the announcement of the COVID-19 pandemic on the number of steps taken by application users was investigated. The fact that the application is easily available worldwide made it possible to obtain data from a huge number of users, exceeding over 450,000 from 187 countries. Analysis of the data collected showed a significant decrease in sports activity among users – within 30 days of the announcement of the pandemic, the number of steps decreased on average by 30%. Due to the accessibility of the platform, very valuable results were obtained – the number of steps and sports activities was regionally dependent and rested on the current state of the pandemic and restrictions. It should be acknowledged that platforms and applications complementing wearables are a superb tool for users; they are especially important in a pandemic situation in which access to medical care is difficult. Analysing basic parameters such as pulse or blood saturation can be essential. Simultaneously, databases from the apps and platforms can be used by researchers to conduct quantitative research on very large, valuable and representative data.

## Contactless payments as a use case

In addition to many sports functions working with the sports platforms and apps, the newest types of wearables also frequently have payment functionalities. Devices such as the Apple Watch, Fitbit Garmin or WearOS smartwatches use NFC (Near Field Communication) technology (Leong, Hew, Tan, & Ooi, 2013). It is an extension of RFID (Radio Field Identification) known from contactless payment cards. NFC payments began to be implemented around 2014 when the revolutionary Host Card Emulation technology created by SimplyTapp was introduced in the newest version of Google's Android operating system. Since then, the NFC-HCE technology has allowed the emulation of a payment card and at the same time payment via a mobile application that uses data stored in the cloud (Pourghomi, Abi-Char, & Ghinea, 2015). It has been applied across mobile banking applications and mobile card wallets around the world, and is equally well used in wearables. With the use of mobile card wallets and apps, users might store credit, debit, prepaid and loyalty cards in one place, substituting for a real wallet. Considering this, the definition of wearable payments proposed by Lee et al. (2020) – that wearable payments are "a form of contactless mobile payment using an NFC-enabled wearable device" – seems reasonable and we adopt this definition for the purposes of this research. Within the first study conducted by Borowski-Beszta & Polasik (2020), a connection between the use of sports and payment functionalities was proved, as there is mutual interaction and stimulation of use between the two groups. It is worth mentioning that other non-sports functions are also important when using wearables. With a complementary sports, payment and lifestyle tool, consumers can use its features constantly.

## The world market of wearable devices

Currently, wrist-worn wearables are becoming increasingly popular. In 2015, a report from Gartner (www1) stated that by 2018 half of the

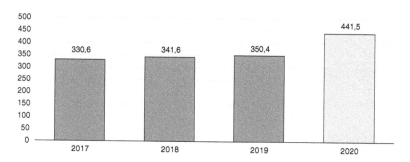

*Figure 6.1* The number of wearable device users worldwide in the years 2017–2020 (millions).

Source: Own elaboration based on: Statista, *Statista Global Consumer Survey*, 2019. *Forecast for the number of users in 2020 adjusted for the expected impact of COVID-19 in May 2020.

users of smartphones on mature markets are likely to use a combination of mobile payments and wearables (Lee et al., 2020). The further potential growth of the wearable market has already been indicated by several researchers, such as Lee et al. (2020); Moon, Baker, & Goughnour, (2019) or Tarabasz and Poddar (2019). Figure 6.1 presents the number of wearable devices users worldwide in the years 2017–2020.

The number of wearable devices users worldwide increases year by year. In 2017, the total was around 331 million. At the end of 2019, the number of wearable devices users was over 350 million and it was expected that 2020 would see it reach almost 357 million. However, forecasts for market development in future years should be cautious. According to a report from March 2020, presented by Statista Research Department, the development of the wearables market will slow down due to the COVID-19 pandemic. The report states that the wearables market grew over 89% in 2019 and the growth dropped to slightly over 9% in 2020. Figure 6.2 presents the approximate age distribution of wearable devices worldwide. At the same time, it should be noted that the popularity of sports platforms is growing dynamically – Strava alone has over 55 million active users who, in just one year (2019–2020), entered over 1 billion activities on the application (Strava, 2020).

According to the report, the largest group of wearables users in the world is people in the 25–34 age range. Interestingly, young people under the age of 25 make up just 14%. This may mean that users of wearables are people who already have access to broadly understood banking services and who also work professionally. Young people aged 18–24 are just entering the payment services market, setting up their

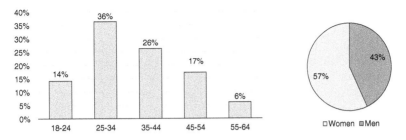

*Figure 6.2* Age and gender distribution among the wearable devices users worldwide.

Source: Own elaboration based on: Statista, *Statista Global Consumer Survey*, 2019.

first bank accounts and then starting to use modern payment services, including payments with wearables. On the other hand, people from age groups over 25 who work professionally mighty look for life balance and quick access to payment services while doing amateur sports – payment-enabled wearable devices can be the answer to their needs.

## Material and methods

The analysis carried out in this work was based on the of the Technology Acceptance Model concept. The Technology Acceptance Model (TAM), presented in 1986 by F. Davis enables explanation of the determinants of the use of a given solution, as well as description of the behaviour of users of various IT systems or technological solutions (Davis, Bagozzi, & Warshaw, 1989). The TAM model has been widely used as a framework for researching wearables (Borowski-Beszta & Polasik, 2020; Chuah et al., 2016; Dehghani, Kim, & Dangelico, 2018; Kim & Chiu, 2019; Kim & Shin, 2015 Rajanen & Weng, 2017; Yildirim & Ali-Eldin, 2019) as well as mobile payment systems (de Luna, Montoro-Ríos, Liébana-Cabanillas, & Montoro-Ríos, 2015; Issa, 2011; Leong et al., 2013; Liébana-Cabanillas, de Luna, & Montoro-Ríosa, 2017; Liébana-Cabanillas, Molinillo, & Ruiz-Montañez, 2019; Patil, Tamilmani, Rana, & Raghavan, 2020; Polasik, Wisniewski, & Lightfoot, 2012).

Within the Technology Acceptance Model, the main assumption is that the acceptance or rejection of a particular technology results from the perception of this technology by potential users. The classic version of the model is based on two main factors: *Perceived Usefulness* (PU) and *Perceived Ease of Use* (PEoU). *Perceived Usefulness* explains the degree to which a user of a given technology believes that the use of a given system or solution can increase work efficiency. The second factor – *Perceived*

*Ease of Use* – can be defined as the degree to which the user believes that the use of a given system or solution is effortless. In this study, individual questions were asked in such a way that the features examined could be classified under the headings of *Perceived Usefulness* and *Perceived Ease of Use*, as well as of *Perceived Security* (PS), which proved to be a valuable extension of TAM in the field of payment devices (Barkhordari, Nourollah, Mashayekhi, Mashayekhi, & Ahangar, 2017; Oliveira, Thomas, Baptista, & Campos, 2016). The research process was divided into two stages of empirical studies. The first stage – quantitative data analysis – used empirical data from a nationwide representative Computer-Assisted Web Interview (CAWI) survey of Internet users in Poland ($N = 1{,}012$), which was conducted in December 2018. The second stage of the process – qualitative data analysis – supplements the conclusions drawn from the quantitative data analysis. It included individual in-depth interviews with 20 participants.

As part of the study, the following research questions were developed:

Q1: What is the popularity of wearable devices among Polish users?

Q2: What is the usage of financial services among wearables users and non-users?

Q3: What is the Perceived Usefulness of NFC payments among wearables users?

Q4: What is the Perceived Ease of Use of NFC payments among wearables users?

Q5: What are the motivations behind the usage of wearable devices and NFC payments among wearables users?

## Results of quantitative data analysis: the survey

Answering the first of the research questions (Q1), the CAWI survey revealed that wrist-worn wearables (smartwatches or smartbands) are used by almost 20% of Polish Internet users (197 out of 1012). Figure 6.3 shows the age and gender distribution of wearable devices users in Poland. This is similar to the findings of the *Statista Global Consumer Survey*. In Poland, the group of users under 25 years of age totals the same percentage as globally (only 14% of the total number). The largest group of wearables users are people aged 25–34 (24%), who could be considered as working professionally and already being established in the payment services market. However, the ranking is similar, i.e. the second most numerous group is people aged 35–44 and the third group is people aged between 45 and 54. It is noteworthy

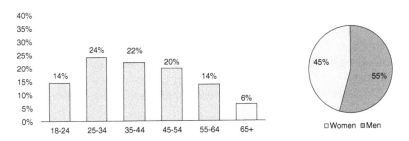

*Figure 6.3* Age and gender distribution among the wearable devices users in
Poland.

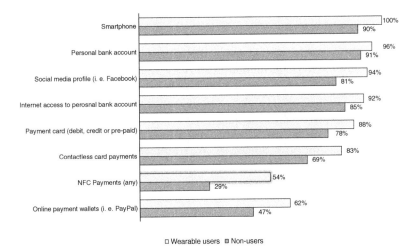

*Figure 6.4* The usage of products and financial services among wearable
devices users and non-users.

that the gender structure is reversed for global statistics – more wearables users in Poland are men. This suggests that Poland is in an earlier
phase than most of the world because men are often the first to engage
with given technological solutions, while women overtake them in a
later phase – as happened in the initial phases of Internet banking in
Poland (Polasik & Wisniewski, 2009).

Figure 6.4 presents the use of selected products and financial services among wearables users and non-users in Poland. Referring to
research question number two (Q2), it turned out that every type of
service is more common among wearables users. About 96% of wearables users have a personal bank account and 92% have Internet access

to their banking account. When it comes to the use of payment cards, over 83% of wearable devices users use contactless card payments, while for non-users the number is visibly lower, below 70%. However, the most significant gap proved to be in the usage of NFC mobile payments. It turned out that more than half of wearables users use NFC payments when only every fourth non-user uses payments of this type. The chart below indicates a higher level of technological and financial advancement among users.

After presenting the availability of products and financial services for wearables users, we examined the use of various types of applications among users and non-users. Banking, health, sport, loyalty and music applications were considered as types of basic applications that are used in everyday life and when doing sports. As for financial services, wearable devices users use mobile apps much more often (Figure 6.5). Three out of four users of wearables use mobile banking applications. Among non-users, it is significantly less, about 45%. Considering wearables as an opportunity for amateur athletes to leave the house without having to take their wallet with them, the result is promising. On the Polish market, mobile banking applications are one of the leading distribution channels for NFC mobile payments. Thus, knowledge of banking applications also allows users to activate digital card wallets for NFC payments. Wearable devices users use sport (43%), music (41%) and health (29%) applications much more often when compared to non-users.

These results are justified because wearables are a hub, which, in conjunction with the smartphone application, makes it easier to practice amateur sport, while moving it to a higher level. Figure 6.6 presents

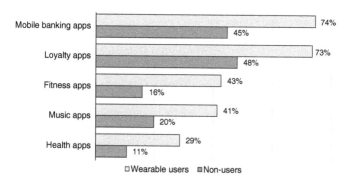

*Figure 6.5* The usage of mobile application types among wearable devices users and non-users.

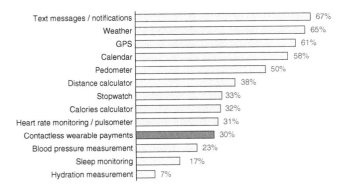

*Figure 6.6* The usage of functionalities of wearables.

the use of individual functionalities by wearables users in Poland. The most commonly used functionality of wearables is checking notifications and text messages. Two of the main sport and health functionalities include a pedometer (50%) and distance measurement (38%). Very similar answers were obtained in relation to a stopwatch (33%), calories burner calculator (32%), and heart rate monitor (31%). It is worth noting that almost every third wearable user conducts payments with the use of NFC payment-enabled wearables. Current restrictions may be related to the characteristics of wearables because not all of them have a payment module. Taking that into consideration, the penetration of wrist-worn wearable payments is high.

In the next step of the analysis of quantitative data, we examined how users of wearables perceive NFC mobile payments in comparison to the non-wearables control group. Survey participants responded to five statements in which they assessed the perceived convenience, speed, ease of use, financial control and security of NFC mobile payments. A five-point Likert scale was used, in which "1" means "strongly disagree" while "5" – "strongly agree." Detailed results have been presented in Figure 6.7.

The above cross-analysis (Figure 6.7) indicated that over 2/3 of users of wearables consider NFC mobile payments convenient. When compared to the control group of non-users, the difference is over 14% in favour of the users. Similar discrepancies were noted for the perceived NFC payments speed, as well as perceived ease of use of NFC mobile payments. Previously analysed data (Figures 6.4 and 6.5) have indicated that not only are wearable payment users more likely to be active sportspeople, they are also likely to be more technologically advanced.

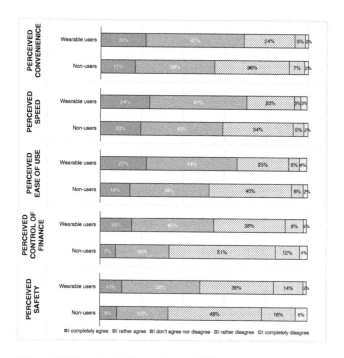

*Figure 6.7* Perceived Convenience (PC), Speed (PS), Ease of Use (PEoU), Control of Finance (PCoF) and Safety (PS) of NFC mobile payments among wearables users and non-users in Poland.

Perceived control over personal finance and perceived security showed the most significant differences between users and non-users of wearables. For individual financial control, more than half of wearables users consider NFC mobile payments a decent personal finance management tool. It means that they have competence to manage their personal finances with the use of NFC payments when compared to non-users. Only 33% of non-wearables users are positive about NFC in this category. In terms of perceived safety, the differences are similar. Again, about half of wearables users indicated that NFC payments are secure; among the non-users, it is every third person.

In conclusion, the results refer to research questions Q3 and Q4. By interpreting them in the context of the TAM research framework, it can be seen that NFC payments are perceived as more useful and easy to use for wearables users than for non-users. The perceived speed and control of finance activities indicated much higher difference in positive indications between the groups of wearable users and non-users.

At the same time, ease of use and convenience have also higher precepts. This suggests that these aspects are essential drivers for wearable devices users to pay with the use of NFC, especially, since speed, convenience and ease of use are vital when while doing sports.

The aspect of financial control is revealed as important among athletes who use NFC payments regularly. This suggests the high usefulness of NFC payments in the context of amateur sport. The security of mobile payments always has lower perceived security than traditional payment methods, which are more sophisticated. However, users of wearables are more technologically aware and still have a greater sense of security when paying with the use of mobile devices.

## Results of qualitative data analysis: the interviews

Conclusions from the analysis of the quantitative survey of Polish Internet users are significantly enhanced by findings from the qualitative research conducted in December 2018, using the IDI (individual in-depth interview) technique. This method is based on the interview moderator's conversation with the respondent on a specific topic, through which it is possible to ascertain individual perspectives on one or more narrowly defined topics. Interviews are conducted with a small sample of respondents and are often used to provide context and refine other data (including quantitative data), while offering a more complete picture of research results. In this study, an interviewer's script, containing detailed topics of conversation and questions to participants, was used. Twenty residents from four cities with populations over 200,000 participated in the interviews (Table 6.1).

Because the study concerns wearable devices, half the participants were active users of wearables (smartwatches or smartbands). Both users and non-users included a group of amateur sportspeople. Because mobile banking applications are the main platform for the distribution

*Table 6.1* Distribution of gender and place of residence of interview participants

| City | Female | Male | Total |
|------|--------|------|-------|
| Toruń | 2 | 5 | 7 |
| Warsaw | 4 | 2 | 6 |
| Bydgoszcz | 2 | 3 | 5 |
| Białystok | 1 | 1 | 2 |
| | 9 | 11 | 20 |

of NFC mobile payments in Poland, regular use of mobile banking applications was adopted as an additional criterion in selecting participants for the study. It was therefore possible to obtain opinions on the usage of wearable devices as well as mobile contactless payments with the use of smartphones and wearables. In analysing qualitative data, the researchers supported their work with the use of the data coding and categorisation assumptions proposed by G. R. Gibbs (2007). Each participant was given a code consisting of three characters in order to anonymise personal data. Two digits are the interview number and a letter indicates the gender of the respondent, where "F" means female and "M" male.

## Usage of wearable devices

In-depth interviews made it possible to obtain answers to questions about the use of interviewees' own wearable devices. Interview analysis revealed the existence of two main categories of response related to the usage of wearable devices:

a   the reasons of usage and functionalities used,
b   the advantages of wearable devices.

The decision to purchase wearables among the respondents was well thought out – the respondents had certain expectations as to the devices they purchased – they did not make a blind purchase and want the devices to support their health or sports activities. Their knowledge about their devices and the wearables market was also relatively extensive. For example, 012M respondent, who does intense amateur sport in the form of triathlons offered a fascinating opinion:

> I would say such a slogan that every self-respecting triathlete has a smartwatch. There are three companies, Garmin, Polar and Suunto. It seems to me that Garmin is the most popular, somewhere Suunto is probably in second place, Polar in third, but, but these watches among triathlonists are very popular. Well, I think that for, for, in principle, for every active person there may be a model of such a watch, but if someone just has such more frequent workouts, well this is a nice element I think for, for everyday workouts and you can actually see it and professional athletes and amateurs also.

Answering research question Q5, the respondents drew attention to the fact that athletes can monitor their training during amateur sports activities, but health reasons were also one of the motives for respondents using wearables. 02F explained that she started using wearables "… for health reasons. […] And I got used to it and already started to use other functions such as measuring distance in the swimming pool, well, various sports." Some were driven by doctors' prescriptions. 05F pointed out that "at the beginning it was a pedometer because I had to increase the number of steps" in order to improve health. Participants who do more advanced amateur sports used complex functionalities and stress tests:

> you determine [the intensity] on a scale of one to five, and this watch, based on heart rate and how much distance we traveled, with what intensity it shows us, how much it challenged our body. In addition, it displays the recommended break time for us.
>
> (12M)

Communication functionalities were also often highlighted by the users of wearables. One of the respondents found it useful not only for reading text messages but also for answering or rejecting phone calls: "if I'm somewhere else and I can't answer [my phone], I have the bell set quite loudly, then if I push it here, it still rings here, but the phone is muted" (019F). Some user interviewees use communication functionalities very extensively. For example 06M, who possessed several different wearable devices, including smartwatches and smartbands, explained that he happens "to have some days that I put my smartphone in my jacket, in my inner pocket and from 10am to 10pm all messages, all conversations, I carry out on my Smartwatch." This indicates that wearable devices are perceived as useful and easy to use when compared to smartphones.

In support of findings from quantitative research and in answer to research questions Q2 and Q3, each user of wearables found advantages in this type of device, pointing out different areas. 12M explained the usefulness of wearable devices when doing amateur sports – running or cycling:

> … this device has these two main advantages. The first is to monitor this activity via GPS and Glonax. So during what interests me, for example, running or cycling, I see the pace, speed at which I run, with which I ride a bike, duration (…). For me, I would mention pulse measurement, it is very important, time measurement, what, what is the pace of a given activity, hm. I also appreciate the algorithm that calculates the value of this effort, how much this activity has challenged us.

The advantages pointed out by interview participants are consistent and focused on having useful and easy to use sports, health and communication functionalities. Most of the group indicated awareness that different wearables offer different types of functionalities. Respondents who used more lifestyle wearables (e.g. 016F) indicated, however, that it is worth noting that sports functions were very developed. On the other hand, users of typically sports watches (e.g. Suunto -02F), indicated that they would happily use a payment functionality if their watch had it. 016F, who is happy with the use of her device, pointed out that

> unfortunately, these devices, they have spread too quickly and everyone has to have one, and to buy good quality, you have to put some money aside. ... I do not believe in devices that perform all functions. I assume that very cool Apple watches are not really good at sports issues. So you know. Something for something.

## Usage of NFC payments

During the second part of the interviews, participants discussed the usage of NFC mobile payments. Based on data obtained from the interviews, it was possible to generate the following categories explaining the attitudes of participants towards payments using a mobile device:

a   the reasons for usage and the advantages of NFC mobile payments,
b   the reasons for not using NFC payments.

In answer to research questions Q3, Q4 and Q5, the main advantages and the reasons for usage of NFC mobile payments were said to be their convenience and speed, which translates into *Perceived Usefulness* and *Ease of Use*. Respondent 06M pointed to several important features of NFC payments for him, one of which is related to the convenient control of personal finance:

> as I pay via NFC, the one built into the phone, the plus is that even on Sunday I get funds charged automatically from the account. It automatically records this transaction. If I had to contactlessly pay by card, it would be recorded up to 3 days later, I would be surprised later, where would 30 PLN disappear? And yes I know right away, because it comes immediately then, because it is then a direct operation on the account. It's so convenient.

NFC payments seem to be a good financial and safe management tool for interview participants. For 04M, who uses wearables, NFC is the best payment solution when doing sports. Changing the NFC payment platform when replacing a smartphone with a device from another company was not a problem.

> Before, I had Samsung, it also supported NFC, so I also used contactless payments. Also it was convenience from the beginning. Oh, for example, maybe – I ride a bike often and as much as possible and it is known that I would not like to carry the card with me. Once, I put the card in the case, in the case, to take it out, pay myself somewhere in the store when I run out of water or something, and you know it's easier with the phone to just go somewhere you want to buy something, you will pay ...

The author of this statement, like many respondents, drew attention to the possibility of replacing the wallet. This feature was one of the main advantages mentioned by women, as indicated by 02F, 07F and 10F respondents.

From a different perspective, the 02F respondent, who possesses a smartwatch without NFC, raised the issue of health – NFC mobile payments successfully replaced a purse with a wallet: "I pay by phone, because I don't carry a purse, my phone is a wallet. Because I can't carry anything." Due to health problems, she uses the phone as a versatile tool for performing various activities, including making payments: "I have only my phone with me. Now I don't even have to have a valid card."

People who regularly use NFC speak highly about this payment solution and indicate the high level of *Perceived Security* of NFC. The key to security is the ability to set different levels and methods of authorisation, including biometric solutions – face or fingerprint identification. According to respondent 03M, "it's safer, really much safer than a standard proximity card, because you have to confirm with a face, face or fingerprint and you can't be accidentally scanned by someone somewhere." Respondent 04M also referred to the biometric authorisation method: "it is also safer, it seems to me, because I do not take out my wallet, nothing will fall out."

Several study participants (05F, 09F, 13F) clearly stated that they do not use this payment method out of habit but would probably be willing to start paying using NFC. Habit was the main reason given by other participants for not using NFC, but they did not rule out using it in future. Interestingly, the benefits of NFC payments have also been noticed by a person who does not use NFC:

regarding NFC, because I do not use [it], but I see the pros. Indeed, there are situations that sometimes that I don't know, someone robs me and I only have the phone for example, no? Well, I really have some last options. Well, it's as if I added another card to the set, an ace up the sleeve, so to speak. And in such critical situations it could really come in handy, if I'm out of cash and my card is gone, or damaged, so I still have a phone.

(13M)

Respondent 13M, who uses wearables but does not use NFC, is aware of the benefits of wearable payments: "I've heard feedback from colleagues that it's very cool that they don't have to think about the wallet."

Summing up these analyses of data from the in-depth interviews with 20 respondents, it is noteworthy that NFC contactless payments are very well regarded by people who use them. Each answer mentioned numerous advantages and a high level of satisfaction with use. What's more, according to the research participants, these payments have been used in various situations – they are universally useful and their advantages have also been noticed by some people not using NFC payments.

## Conclusions

Studies have confirmed that financial services, in particular contactless payments, have an important role in amateur sport among wearables users. The ability to make NFC payments using smartphones is already perceived as a useful tool for people using wearables. With the continuous developments in wearables technology, the quality of sports training visibly improves as, thanks to these devices, users can conduct financial transactions with the use of devices worn on their wrists. These devices are particularly useful in the case of amateur athletes who train on their own. There is no question of being able to have a wallet to hand during training sessions and people also tend to leave their smartphones at home or in the changing room. With payment-enabled wearables, users can use both sport and financial functionalities and manage scheduled or unexpected payments, for example paying for return transport.

Studies have shown the validity of the Technology Acceptance Model for wearables in sports and payment services. Within this study, the *Perceived Usefulness* of wearables for conducting contactless payments at retail stores was demonstrated in both quantitative and qualitative research. This method of analysis has enabled the understanding of detailed aspects and motivations of usage of NFC payments by wearables users. In the quantitative research, both *Perceived Usefulness* and *Perceived Ease of Use* were confirmed as important stimuli for using NFC payments. In the qualitative research stage, interview participants confirmed the initial conclusions of the quantitative study.

The results of the study indicate that the popularity of wearable NFC payments will probably increase, while payment and sports platforms can contribute to its popularisation. Wearables seem to have a massive potential for users who are familiar with this type of payment, as well as for the 70% of wearables users who have not made wearable contactless payments before. With the popularisation of NFC-equipped devices, payment-enabled wearables can become a standard and integral accessory of active people who do sports. An interesting aspect for future studies is the combination of sports training with mobile financial services, especially in real-time, as well as of telematic-based insurance with the use of wearables.

## Acknowledgements

This work was supported by the National Science Centre, Poland under Grant No. 2017/26/E/HS4/00858.

## Bibliography

Barkhordari, M., Nourollah, Z., Mashayekhi, H., Mashayekhi, Y., & Ahangar, M. S. (2017). Factors influencing adoption of e-payment systems: An empirical study on Iranian customers. *Information Systems and E-Business Management*, *15*(1), 89–116. https://doi.org/10.1007/s10257-016-0311-1

Borowski-Beszta, M., & Polasik, M. (2020). Wearable devices: New quality in sports and finance. *Journal of Physical Education and Sport*, *20*(2), 1077–1084. https://doi.org/10.7752/jpes.2020.s2150

Chuah, S. H. W., Rauschnabel, P. A., Krey, N., Nguyen, B., Ramayah, T., & Lade, S. (2016). Wearable technologies: The role of usefulness and visibility in smartwatch adoption. *Computers in Human Behavior*, *65*(October 2017), 276–284. https://doi.org/10.1016/j.chb.2016.07.047

Davis, F. D., Bagozzi, R. P., & Warshaw, P. R. (1989). User acceptance of computer technology: A comparison of two theoretical models. *Management Science*, *35*(8), 982–1003. https://doi.org/10.1287/mnsc.35.8.982

de Luna, R., Montoro-Ríos, F., Liébana-Cabanillas, F., & Montoro-Ríos, F. (2015). Determinants of the intention to use NFC technology as a payment system: An acceptance model approach. *Information Systems and E-Business Management*, *14*(2), 293–314. https://doi.org/10.1007/s10257-015-0284-5

Dehghani, M., Kim, K. J., & Dangelico, R. M. (2018). Will smartwatches last? Factors contributing to intention to keep using smart wearable technology.

*Telematics and Informatics, 35*(2), 480–490. https://doi.org/10.1016/j.tele. 2018.01.007

Gibbs, G. R. (2007). *Analysing Qualitative Data.* London: Sage Publications.

Guk, K., Han, G., Lim, J., Jeong, K., Kang, T., Lim, E. K., & Jung, J. (2019). Evolution of wearable devices with real-time disease monitoring for personalised healthcare. *Nanomaterials, 9*(6), 1–23. https://doi.org/10.3390/nano9060813

Issa, H. (2011). Assessment and user adoption of NFC in comparison to other mobile payments systems. *SSRN Electronic Journal.* https://doi. org/10.2139/ssrn.1910471

Kheirkhahan, M., Nair, S., Davoudi, A., Rashidi, P., Wanigatunga, A. A., Corbett, D. B., ... Ranka, S. (2019). A smartwatch-based framework for real-time and online assessment and mobility monitoring. *Journal of Biomedical Informatics, 89*(November 2018), 29–40. https://doi.org/10.1016/j. jbi.2018.11.003

Kim, K. J., & Shin, D.-H. (2015). An acceptance model for smart watches. *Internet Research, 25*(4), 527–541. https://doi.org/10.1108/IntR-05-2014-0126

Kim, T., & Chiu, W. (2019). Consumer acceptance of sports wearable technology: The role of technology readiness. *International Journal of Sports Marketing and Sponsorship, 20*(1), 109–126. https://doi.org/10.1108/IJSMS-06-2017-0050

Lee, V. H., Hew, J. J., Leong, L. Y., Tan, G. W. H., & Ooi, K. B. (2020). Wearable payment: A deep learning-based dual-stage SEM-ANN analysis. *Expert Systems with Applications, 157*, 113–477. https://doi.org/10.1016/j. eswa.2020.113477

Leong, L.-Y., Hew, T.-S., Tan, G. W.-H., & Ooi, K.-B. (2013). Predicting the determinants of the NFC-enabled mobile credit card acceptance: A neural networks approach. *Expert Systems with Applications, 40*(14), 5604–5620. https://doi.org/10.1016/j.eswa.2013.04.018

Liébana-Cabanillas, F., de Luna, I. R., & Montoro-Ríosa, F. (2017). Intention to use new mobile payment systems: A comparative analysis of SMS and NFC payments. *Economic Research-Ekonomska Istrazivanja, 30*(1), 892–910. https://doi.org/10.1080/1331677X.2017.1305784

Liébana-Cabanillas, F., Molinillo, S., & Ruiz-Montañez, M. (2019). To use or not to use, that is the question: Analysis of the determining factors for using NFC mobile payment systems in public transportation. *Technological Forecasting and Social Change, 139*(March 2018), 266–276. https://doi.org/ 10.1016/j.techfore.2018.11.012

Lim, J. S., Noh, G-Y., (2017) Effects of gain-versus loss-framed performance feedback on the use of fitness apps: Mediating role of exercise self-efficacy and outcome expectations of exercise, *Computers in Human Behavior,* (77), 249–257, https://doi.org/10.1016/j.chb.2017.09.006.

Moon, N. W., Baker, P. M., & Goughnour, K. (2019). Designing wearable technologies for users with disabilities: Accessibility, usability, and connectivity factors. *Journal of Rehabilitation and Assistive Technologies Engineering, 6*, 205566831986213. https://doi.org/10.1177/2055668319862137

Oliveira, T., Thomas, M., Baptista, G., & Campos, F. (2016). Mobile payment: Understanding the determinants of customer adoption and intention to recommend the technology. *Computers in Human Behavior, 61*(2016), 404–414. https://doi.org/10.1016/j.chb.2016.03.030

Ollander, S., Godin, C., Campagne, A., & Charbonnier, S. (2017). A comparison of wearable and stationary sensors for stress detection. *2016 IEEE International Conference on Systems, Man, and Cybernetics, SMC 2016—Conference Proceedings,* (March 2019), 4362–4366. https://doi.org/10.1109/SMC.2016.7844917

Patil, P., Tamilmani, K., Rana, N. P., & Raghavan, V. (2020). Understanding consumer adoption of mobile payment in India: Extending Meta-UTAUT model with personal innovativeness, anxiety, trust, and grievance redressal. *International Journal of Information Management, 54*(May), 102144. https://doi.org/10.1016/j.ijinfomgt.2020.102144

Polasik, M., & Wisniewski, T. P. (2009). Empirical analysis of internet banking adoption in Poland. *International Journal of Bank Marketing, 27*(1), 32–52. https://doi.org/10.1108/02652320910928227

Polasik, M., Wisniewski, T. P., & Lightfoot, G. (2012). Modelling customers' intentions to use contactless cards. *International Journal of Banking, Accounting and Finance, 4*(3), 203–231. https://doi.org/10.1504/IJBAAF.2012.051590

Pourghomi, P., Abi-Char, P. E., & Ghinea, G. (2015). Analysis of host card emulation and secure element. *International Journal of Computer Science and Information Security, 13*(12), 156–164.

Rajanen, D., & Weng, M. (2017). Digitisation for fun or reward? A study of acceptance of wearable devices for personal healthcare. *Proceedings of the 21st International Academic Mindtrek Conference, AcademicMindtrek 2017, 2017–JANUA.* https://doi.org/10.1145/3131085.3131118

Rivers, D. J., (2020) Strava as a discursive field of practice: Technological affordances and mediated cycling motivations, *Discourse, Context & Media,* (34) https://doi.org/10.1016/j.dcm.2019.100345.

Tarabasz, A., & Poddar, G. (2019). Factors influencing adoption of wearable devices in Dubai. *Journal of Economics and Management, 36*(2), 123–143. https://doi.org/10.22367/jem.2019.36.07

Thorp, E. O. (1998). The invention of the first wearable computer. *International Symposium on Wearable Computers, Digest of Papers, 1998–October* (June 1999), 4–8. https://doi.org/10.1109/ISWC.1998.729523

Tison, G. H., Avram, R., Kuhar, P., Abreau, S., Marcus, G. M., Pletcher, M. J, & Olgin, J. E. (2020). Worldwide effect of COVID-19 on physical activity: A descriptive study. *Annals of Internal Medicine, 173*(9), 767–770. https://doi.org/10.7326/M20-2665

Wang, K.-L. (2015). Application of wearable devices to running during training. *International Journal of Machine Learning and Computing, 5*(6), 445–449. https://doi.org/10.18178/ijmlc.2015.5.6.549

Yildirim, H., & Ali-Eldin, A. M. T. (2019). A model for predicting user intention to use wearable IoT devices at the workplace. *Journal of King Saud University – Computer and Information Sciences, 31*(4), 497–505. https://doi.org/10.1016/j.jksuci.2018.03.001

(www1) Gartner, *Gartner Says By 2018, 50 Percent of Consumers in Mature Markets Will Use Smartphones or Wearables for Mobile Payments*, https:// www.gartner.com/en/newsroom/press-releases/2015-12-15-gartner-says-by-2018-50-percent-of-consumers-in-mature-markets-will-use-smartphones-or-wearables-for-mobile-payments

(www2) Statista, *Statista Global Consumer Survey 2019*, https://www.statista.com/outlook/319/100/wearables/worldwide

(www3) Statista, *Impact of coronavirus (COVID-19) outbreak on global wearables market growth forecast in 2019, 2020 and 2024*, https://www.statista.com/statistics/1106297/worldwide-wearables-market-growth-impacted-by-covid-19-outbreak/#statisticContainer

(www4) *T-Mobile*, https://kilometrami.pl/

(www5) *Google Play*, https://play.google.com/

(www6) Strava, *Strava Milestones: 50 Million Athletes and 3 Billion Activity Uploads*, https://blog.strava.com/press/strava-milestones-50-million-athletes-and-3-billion-activity-uploads/

# Conclusion

In describing digital business models in sport, it is important to be aware that they are not just a successor to traditional business models. They are better defined as an extended version of the traditional model, taking into account the trajectory of sports enterprises towards digital transformation. This understanding is linked to a better representation of the advantages of using digital business models, which are most often seen as related to value creation based on data processing methods (such as statistical analysis of players, fan movement analysis, e-ticketing). Such an understanding is mainly related to the creation of new (equally important) ways of doing sports business.

Obviously, the aspects of digital business models in sport presented in this publication should be treated as an introduction to the topic and not as a comprehensive overview. It is certainly worth looking at a future in the context of creating models based on the idea of Marketing 4.0 or digital marketing supported by information and communication technologies, including the use of influencers to create new content in social media (TikTok, Instagram) or Twitch – a platform focused on gaming on which, for example, interviews with players are posted (Ibai Llanos, known simply as 'Ibai' conducted the first interview with Leo Messi when he moved to Paris Saint-Germain on Twitch). That example also shows that business models are not only implemented by sports organisations but can be guided by the athletes themselves, and in this case digitalisation shows how big it can be in creating powerful personal brands.

Having talked about Twitch, we must not forget about e-sports, which are also increasingly penetrating the world of real sports. E-sports events such as the Formula 1® Esports Series or the e-sports sections of football clubs such as Ajax Amsterdam are designed not only to increase the number of young fans but also to expand the brand, which in the virtual world no longer has any borders. This expansion,

DOI: 10.4324/9781003270126-8

in addition to creating a new way to engage fans, also translates into additional streaming revenues as well as new sponsorships.

To sum up, the digitisation of sports organisations can be considered from two perspectives – the first influencing the performance of athletes (data analysis), while the second is related to sports club management, including the creation of new fan experiences. An example of this is the blockchain-based Socios.com platform, which encourages fans of football, basketball and hockey teams (*e.g.*, FC Barcelona, Paris Saint-Germain, Chicago Bulls) to buy and sell club fan tokens.

A number of issues around digital transformation in sport, including the still not fully exploited potential for value creation in the virtual world show that the trend towards digitalisation is not a passing fad, but a challenge for sports organisations in the years to come.

# Index

Note: **Bold** page numbers refer to tables and *italic* page numbers refer to figures.

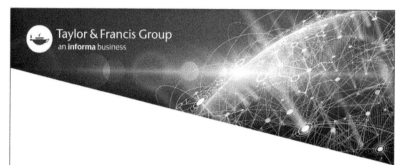